Robert Collyer

The Life That Now Is

Sermons

Robert Collyer

The Life That Now Is
Sermons

ISBN/EAN: 9783744743228

Printed in Europe, USA, Canada, Australia, Japan

Cover: Foto ©Lupo / pixelio.de

More available books at **www.hansebooks.com**

THE LIFE THAT NOW IS:

SERMONS

BY

ROBERT COLLYER,

AUTHOR OF "NATURE AND LIFE."

BOSTON:
HORACE B. FULLER,
14 BROMFIELD STREET.
1871.

Entered, according to Act of Congress, in the year 1871,
BY HORACE B. FULLER,
In the Office of the Librarian of Congress, at Washington.

Stereotyped at the Boston Stereotype Foundry,
No. 19 Spring Lane.

TO

WILLIAM HENRY FURNESS,

WHOSE LIFE IS HID WITH CHRIST IN GOD,

I DEDICATE THIS BOOK.

PREFACE.

The name I have given to this little volume, is also the best preface. It is a selection of such sermons as I have been able to preach about the life that now is. If I thought that any apology was needed for saying so little about that which is to come, I would make this twofold plea: First, that so many better and wiser men have said so much about it already; and, second, I am so sure that if we can but find the right way through this world, and walk in it, the doors of Heaven are as sure to open to us as ours open to our own children when they come eagerly home from school.

R. C.

Chicago, May 9, 1871.

CONTENTS.

CHAPTER		PAGE
I.	Vines and Branches.	1
II.	The Thorn in the Flesh.	23
III.	Every Man a Penny.	49
IV.	The Two Harvests.	67
V.	How Enoch walked with God.	88
VI.	Holiness of Helpfulness.	111
VII.	Gashmu.	137
VIII.	Storming Heaven.	161
IX.	Why Herod feared John.	186
X.	Marriage.	206
XI.	Children and Childhood.	228
XII.	Tender, Trusty, and True.	251
XIII.	Patience.	265
XIV.	The Two Mites.	284
XV.	Old Age.	303
XVI.	At the Soldiers' Graves.	325

SERMONS.

I.

VINES AND BRANCHES.

JOHN xv. 5: "I am the vine, ye are the branches: He that abideth in me, and I in him, the same bringeth forth much fruit: for without me ye can do nothing."

IT is entirely probable that these words were spoken in the spring-time, when the vines on the slopes and terraces about Jerusalem were opening into leaf and blossom, and when this analogy would have all the power and beauty that could come from the object as well as the subject. There, right before them, and all about them, are the vines, standing in the sun. Some of the branches are the genuine outgrowth of the vine itself. Others are only there by grafting. Some are strong, some feeble, and some dead; and the dead, as Jesus is speaking, the vine-dressers are cutting away, that they may not interfere with the living vines or disfigure the vineyards. But, strong, or feeble, or dead, there stand the stems, ready to pour their sap into every branch alike, or, if they make any difference, to give their life to the lowliest first and in the fullest measure, that they which have the less sun may have the more sap, and more at least of life, if they have less of what makes life a blessing. So Jesus said, "I am the vine, ye are the branches, and my Father is the husbandman; and every branch in me that beareth not fruit he taketh away; and every branch that beareth fruit he pruneth it, that it may bear more fruit. Abide in me, and I in you; for as the branch cannot bear fruit of itself, except it abide in the vine, no more can ye, except ye abide in me."

In this sermon I want to try to find this subject through the object, to see how the analogy is true, first naturally, second spiritually, and third universally; how it will hold good while vines and men continue to grow on the earth. It is not something once done, and then done with, but something that is *now doing*, and that will be done to the end of time. In many great, true ways, living stems are still standing in the sun, with their branches strong, or feeble, or dead, about them; and the dead are still cut away, and the living pruned by the husbandman, watching and working forever in this vineyard and among the vines which he has planted.

This truth of the vines and the branches is to be understood, first of all, in a natural sense; and we are to set aside, when we look at it in this sense, what we are fond of calling mystery, but ought rather to call obscurity, and to understand that Jesus meant, first, by what he said then, that these men, sitting or standing about him that day, were to be as intimately united to him through their spirits as the branches are united to the vine — were to draw their highest life through him from God, as these branches drew their sap through the stem from the earth, and were to drink in the sun and make the stem glorious by their fruitfulness, as did these branches on the vine; or, to demonstrate their deadness, in contrast with those that did drink in the sun and bear great clusters, and so fail to be what they might be, not because the sap refused to run and the sun to shine, but because they did not turn sap and sun to good account by bringing forth good fruit.

So that the power by which Jesus first drew Peter and John to his side, and held them there, was a personal and perfectly natural power; and we are not to think of it as a mystery, except as the influence of one life and soul over another for good or evil is always a mystery. Attracted to him, this one from his tax-gathering, and that one from his fishing, they had gradually felt the influence of his spirit running through their whole life; were never quite what they ought to be when he did not inspire them; they had no such power to live by as that which in some way they felt flowing out of his nature into theirs; and so they came in the end to see what he meant when he said, "Without me ye can do nothing." If you take a cutting from a feeble stalk, and graft it on a vigorous stem, the books say the result will be that the graft will show a far greater vigor than it could have shown ungrafted; will reveal in fruit or flower, very clearly, the new stock from which it draws its vitality. It was so with these men.

They felt their life grow strong and good in the strength and goodness of their great Friend, and they were to feel it forever, more intensely as the years went on; then they were to send out and take in new branches in their turn; and so the true vine is at last to cover the whole earth. But whether in the world of the apostles, or in the world here and now; in the way Jesus saved Peter, or in the way you are to save the blasphemer, who loves you and is influenced by you as he is by no other man, it is always the lesser growing better by the greater; the weaker being grafted into, and drawing life from, the stronger; the Son of Man forever saved, and sanctified, and fitted for heaven by the Son of God.

So it is well worth our notice that this is, in a great general sense, a prime principle in life; and that, whatever we may say about our individual freedom, the great majority of us are only free as the branch on the vine is free; away back we join into some other personal life for our salvation, and draw from it, as the branch from the stem, our most essential vitality and power — that in a body or in a book, which is the spiritual body of the inspired thinker, some soul, larger and stronger than our own, has got hold of us, and is pouring into us its life, and moulding us this very day.

When Carlyle gave his address in Edinburgh, some years ago, the great hall was filled, not with Scotchmen alone, but with men who poured in from the most distant parts of England and Europe to sit at his feet and drink in his words, because he is to them the vine, and they are the branches. When Mr. Emerson comes to our city, there are those sitting about his feet that will hardly listen to any other living man, because he is to them the vine, and they are the branches. When the gracious and good English queen was left a widow, she found that her life was so interwoven with the life she had lost from her side, as to bring an abandonment of sorrow such as the world has seldom witnessed, so sad it was and heavy; because, though she was queen and he was consort, he was the vine and she was the branch. So Elijah was the vine to Elisha, and David to Jonathan, and Paul to Timothy, and Socrates to Plato; and the world is full of those vines and branches, because it is a natural law of our life. I meet every day men and women who feel that without Channing, or Parker, or Swedenborg, or Wesley, they can do nothing. The great soul has taken them in, and imparted its life to theirs. You may see, sometimes, a young man who will do no good at all until he gets a wife; but then he does really become a man. Now, such a man may scoff at the woman question, as such men sometimes do, and say the common platitudes about the inferiority of the woman's nature to that of the man, as such men often will; but a woman like that is replying, in her silent, steady life, all day long, "I am the vine, you are the branch, and without me you can do nothing." "I consider," says Dr. Arnold, "beyond all wealth, honor, or even health, is the attachment we form to noble souls; because to become one with the good, generous, and true, is to be, in a measure, good, generous, and true yourself."

Now it follows, of course, that this which is at once so natural and universal, must be so far right; because all wrong is unnatural, and, as I am compelled to believe, exceptional. But then it brings up this question: What life, in a body or a book, in earth or in heaven, is the one that can make the most of me, can do most for me, and inspire me to do most for mankind? Can Webster and Hamilton, in political ideas? In commercial morality, can the Lawrences and Hoveys? Can Channing, Parker, or Swedenborg be supreme to me among men in faith, or Emerson in nature, or Tennyson in a far-reaching and delicate intuition? Let me never be suspected of a want of reverence for a noble gift, for a sweet mastery for good, from whatever source it may come. William Furness, writing me once about the distinction made in a new Life of Jesus between the human and divine in his nature, said, "I regret the distinction, because Jesus is the *most* human being that ever lived, and therefore the most divine. His divinity lay in his pure humanity." It is what I think of in this personal relation of the vine and branches in the person of Jesus Christ. I have no need to go into mystery, except I say the mystery that must always dwell in the way one soul inspires another and lives in it. I am simply to realize that if I can become united to Jesus Christ, as the branch is united to the vine, then I become a part of a life, before which Webster and Hamilton pale in their grasp of the principles we have embodied in our Declaration of Independence; who was deeper in the doctrine of the fatherhood than Channing, and understood free grace in a way to make Wesley a dreamer; and before whom princes of commercial morality stand with bared heads as they see the great guiding lines of the Sermon on the Mount.

> "One who, because he overcomes us so
> Because he is most noble, and a king,
> Can well prevail against our fears, and fling
> His purple round us, till our hearts do grow
> So close against his heart as not to know
> How weak they are alone."

This brings me, secondly, to the true test of this union with Christ, what it is, and how it is to be distinguished, or, in other words, the spiritual truth of the analogy.

And I need not take much time telling you, to begin with, that it is a very common thing for every great branch on this Christian stem to claim to be *the* true branch of the true vine. The Romanist bases this claim apparently on being the oldest branch, and the Rationalist on being the newest; the Baptist on being the branch nearest the water, the Quaker on being so far away; the Universalist, because it gets so much sunlight, and the Calvinist, seemingly, because it gets so little; the Episcopalian, because every twig on its particular branch is trained and confirmed in a particular way, and the Unitarian, because each of its sprays is left very much to its natural instinct to grow as it will. And all these claims, as you know, have involved the Christian world in endless, and sometimes shameful, persecutions. Now, will not this analogy of the vine and the branches cast precisely the light we need across the spiritual claims of the church and the man, and light up the whole question of what it is to share in this intimate life of Christ in a way that is never to be mistaken? Suppose the branches on a vine could make this claim that is made by the churches — that one could cry, "Believe in me, for I am the oldest branch;" and another, "In me, for I am the newest;" and this, "In me, for I am most in the sun;" what would be the natural and inevitable reply? There is but one, it is this: you are all alike in being branches on the one stem. But you are not united in this way merely to be most in the water or the sun; it is not a prime question, whether you are the oldest or the newest branch; the sole thing to know is, what fruit do you bear, and how does that fruit compare with what the other branches are bearing? If this branch out in the sun, or this that rejoices in its freedom, shall bear only a few dried-up specimens, while that near the water, or that away back in the shadow, is burdened to breaking, and that tied fast to ecclesiastical trellis-work wholly covers the trellises with its great ripe clusters, then the fruit-bearers are the true branches. If Calvinism can fill a man with love, joy, peace, long-suffering, gentleness, patience, and goodness; if it can send him out to clothe the naked, feed the hungry, visit the sick, pity the prisoner, and to break every yoke, while my faith, or any other, can only inspire me to tell handsomely and eloquently how it is done, but then to leave the real thing undone; to bring out beautiful blossoms that will fill a whole valley with perfume, but to let the blossom suffice and bear no fruit, the world does not hold a more empty boast than mine of being the true branch of the true vine.

But now let us put this just the other way. Suppose a man, making not the least pretension to any intimate union with this vine, one who says, "I know nothing about your claim, that before I can be what I ought to be I must be called after some special dogma, and in some way realize what you hold to be so essential to a fruitful life,—but there is my life itself." And suppose you should see that such a man really does live well; that his life is good, his soul's large windows free from blemish; that he *is* loving, long-suffering, gentle, patient, and good; that the wan face of sickness lights up in his presence, and he is feet to the lame, and a father to the poor, and breaks the bond of oppression, and causes the widows to sing for joy; what would you say to a man like that? You would say, "My friend, when Jesus was here among men, he said, 'other sheep I have, that are not of this fold.'" Now, it is no matter to me that you disclaim this personal union; you hold it all the same. You are one of the branches of the true vine, because you bear good fruit. It would really make no deep and abiding difference if you should say you do not believe in Christ. Christ believes in you, and has gone to prepare a place for you, and will come again, and take you to himself. For a real belief is not some mere opinion, this way or that, in the mind. It is the whole set and purpose of the life and soul; so you can say, "I never taught in the streets in thy name;" but he will say, "You taught the freedman, or sent a teacher to do it." You can deny that you ever cast out devils; but he will say, "Don't you remember that man you picked up out of the gutter, and how you held on to him until he sat clothed and in his right mind? Ye did it unto the least of mine; ye did it to me."

But then it would be a very great mistake to claim that a man, living such a life, and disclaiming Christian ideas and convictions for what he was, and what he was doing, was, therefore, an independent vine of himself; owed nothing to the sap that flows forever from that inexhaustible stock in these Christian lands, and was the growth of a plant whose seed was altogether *in* itself. It is indeed seldom that this is so.

When a man lives a noble life, thinks great thoughts, does great things, shames Christian men by the intrinsic beauty and grace of his life, and yet disclaims connection with the Christian stock, I want to know how he has come into life; and, if he is the son of an unbroken succession of Christian ministers and men running directly through many generations, I say, then, that goes a long way to account for it. You are not a graft, but a natural branch of the great vine. It is true that you are able to live isolated from the special Christian line in the world to-day, but it is very doubtful indeed whether you could have done so well if your fathers had not lived in the Christian church of yesterday. And if a man in my city says to me, "I do not care for churches and worship; I can worship at home;" and then goes on to tell me how his good old father, the deacon, used to go to church in New England, I feel like saying, "My friend, your father, the deacon, I suppose, left you very little money, but he left you a grand legacy of thought and feeling, that reaches up to heaven, and belongs there. The truth is, you are a birthright member of the Christian church. Away back you reach into the true vine. Now you have made your little legacy of money into a fortune, and may the Lord make you the happier for every dollar you are worth. But tell me now, how is it about that other legacy? Are you merely using up the interest of that, or are you dipping into the principal? Is the way you are living likely to end in your children's having such a treasure of the thought and feeling that ennoble the soul as you had, or, in giving them more money, will you give them less grace? Nay, man, make it a personal matter. Tell me what your home worship is doing for the world's salvation, what good fruit comes from it, and then I will tell you exactly what it is worth. For, if it bring the good fruits of the spirit and life that always come of any genuine worship of God whatever, your course is the next best to that of plunging heart and soul into some real Christian church and movement, such as would best answer to your longing and the world's welfare. But if in your isolation you bear no such fruit, and are aware of an ever-slackening endeavor to do anything noble and good, then, I do not doubt that you are still a branch of the great vine; but every branch that beareth not fruit, He taketh away."

But with these illustrations of what a far-reaching influence this of Christ is to us all, and in the most direct way, and what a strict account it holds with every branch on the stem, I say fearlessly, that this one test is the true test, and there is no other of union with Christ, or how I may know and prove it. I bear fruit, or I do not bear fruit; it is good, or it is not good. When that one thing is made clear, the problem is solved so far as I am concerned. Wherever you find a man bearing good fruit, there, whether he may know it or not, in a direct personal way, you find a man united to Jesus Christ,— a true branch of the true vine. I care not what you call him.

And so it is once more, that just as on the vine there is a vast complicated, yet perfect inter-action of one branch on another, as no one branch can possibly exist for itself, but draws in the sunlight to send it down and through the whole vine, sharing what it has got with the others, and sharing what they have got, giving them strength, and getting strength from them; a separate branch in every way, and yet in every way a part of the whole vine, so all these great churches, interests, and influences we call Christian, and know to be such, blend beautifully under all their differences and make the perfect whole. It is like what I experienced in Paris once. I wanted to hear Coquerel, the great French preacher, or at least to see his face, so I went with a brother preacher to his church. We found he was not to be there, and it was not church time. But groping along a dark passage in the basement of the building in the direction of some sounds, we came at last to a door, which opened right into a Sunday school, of at least four hundred children. We sat down quietly during the lesson. I did not understand a word they said. When it was over, they prepared to sing. The superintendent gave the hymn. I was still in the dark, until all at once the whole school burst out into one of the most familiar melodies we use in our own Sunday school, one I had heard in Unity Church a hundred times, and then I seemed to understand all about it. It was like that old Pentecost, long ago, when the Spirit came down, and every man heard the disciples talking in his own tongue. So we say our own words in our own tongue, and are very careful not to get mixed up with others that are saying other words in other tongues, and we hardly understand each other at all. But some day we find a strange congregation at their worship or their work, and though we do not know the words, when they strike the same great chord we are instantly in the whole spirit of the thing, and feel quite at home to the music. It is like the Portuguese Hymn, that is just as good, and gracious, and sweet when it rings in a prayer-meeting, as when it goes swelling and sounding through the grand mass. It is like the hymn-books we use in our worship, written by old saints of the Primitive Church, and saints in the church of to-day; by men and women, those whose hearts were breaking for sorrow, and those whose hearts could hardly hold their own for joy; by men as wide apart as St. Gregory and George Dawson of Birmingham.

> "But they are all made one in Christ,
>   And love each other tenderly,
> The old, the young, the rich, the poor
>   In that great company.
> And there shall come a glorious day,
>   When all the good saints, every one
> Shall meet within their Father's home,
>   And stand before his throne."

And then again, as in the vine the stem makes the branches strong with its strength, fills them with life out of its heart and supplies the sap, the one prime condition of their fruitfulness; and they, in their turn, cover not themselves alone, but the stem also with glory, in the great ripe clusters they bear for the harvest; so in this true vine, the spirit of Christ, out of which the life of the world comes pouring in a never-ceasing stream, the branches can cover the stem itself with glory and praise.

In Manchester, right in the heart of the vast modern city, you find a place two hundred years old, as quiet and still as if there were not a factory within a hundred miles. It includes a noble library of books, to which the whole world has free access, and a foundation in which a great number of boys are educated and fitted for life. More than two hundred years ago Humphrey Chetham died in Manchester; he was a rich man, and left his riches to found this college and library; and there, from that time to this, through all the changes of time in England, forty or more poor boys have been housed and fed, educated and fitted out for life, and that great library of books has been as free as the air to all who wanted to read them. Now think what glory and praise have come in those centuries to that good name in the good this legacy to Manchester has done; how all the world over, men have lived well and wisely, who could say, "I was one of the college boys in Manchester, and had free access to that library, and its nurture and protection made me a man, when I might have been a mere waif and weed in the great highway of the world!" It touches my final idea of this great, true vine, that Jesus, who once entered into the heavens, left to the world this legacy, by which he is and is to be more intensely and gloriously present in his risen life than he was when Peter and John sat by his side in Galilee, as Humphrey Chetham is more intensely and gloriously in Manchester, now two hundred and thirteen years after his death, than ever he was in his life.

O, friends, we read these new Lives of Christ that are pouring from the press! We are fascinated by Renan, and bewildered by Strauss. We get a glimpse of his presence in Ecce Homo, touch the hem of his garments in Schenkel, and almost see him as he was in Furness, and think how glad we should have been to be near him in his very living presence — to be one of the

Twelve, and hear his voice, and touch his hand, and be healed by his power, and lifted by his spirit to God. I tell you this identification is better than that intercourse — to be one with this great vine, as it now lives on this earth; to be one of the branches that draw their life from that vine, that catch the sunlight and rain, grow gloriously towards the heavens, ripen great clusters of fruit, and make the stem glorious in their glory,— this is to know Christ. We cannot read the life of Christ so as to understand it, until we enter into its spirit, any more than Jefferson Davis can understand the life of Abraham Lincoln. Loyalty to Christ's spirit and work is the best commentary, and the only one that can make Christ altogether clear to us. Go about the Father's business as he did. Send his Gospel far and wide ; be ye saviours in your degree; take Christ into your hearts, and then there will be very little trouble about him in your minds. But then never forget that if he is the vine, God is the sun.

There is an awful and unspeakable distinction between the two natures. They can never be the same. He is the true vine, and the whole church

— all true, fruitful souls — are the branches. Yet as vine and branch alike would be nothing without the rain and sun, so even this most blessed life of Christ in the soul would be nothing without God, his Father and our Father — God over all, blessed forevermore!

II.

THE THORN IN THE FLESH.

2 CORINTHIANS xii. 7-9: "And lest I should be exalted above measure through the abundance of the revelations, there was given to me a thorn in the flesh, the messenger of Satan to buffet me, lest I should be exalted above measure. For this thing I besought the Lord thrice, that it might depart from me. And he said unto me, My grace is sufficient for thee: for my strength is made perfect in weakness. Most gladly therefore will I rather glory in my infirmities, that the power of Christ may rest upon me."

WHAT is known in sacred biography as Paul's thorn in the flesh, has been a thorn in the pulpit expositions of all the Christian ages. Carefully concealing its nature himself, he has thereby set all that want to be wise above what is written, in a state of uneasiness to find it out. The result, as might be expected, has been very curious and quite inconclusive. One commentator is clear it was a defect of the eyes; another is certain it was a defect in the speech; and lameness has been supposed, and neuralgia, and a want of that dignity of appearance that is supposed to be indispensable to a successful minister; and so almost endlessly, as different men have been led by different fancies, to this or that conclusion.

So I suppose it cannot be of much use to us to know exactly what this thorn was, since the man who suffered from it did not care to tell us. He certainly cannot have meant to put preachers into the perplexity that has come of his concealment. He may have felt it was too delicate a thing to be made a matter of common talk, even to the brethren, as most persons do who are in Paul's case. Be that as it may, he felt it was right to say that the thorn was there, and he could not get rid of it; could not pray it out, or cry it out, or believe it out, or tear it out, or get the Lord to take it out. There the thorn was, whatever it was, and there it would stay, very likely, to the end of this mortal life. But then he found in the struggle to be free from the thorn, what in the end was better than any such freedom,—power and patience to bear his pain; still the power was not his own, nor the patience, only the thorn. But this was the end of it: the two things together carried him right to God, and laid him to rest in the arms of the Eternal. And as a sick child rests in the arms of its mother, unable to shake off the pain, but still wonderfully supported and comforted out of her love, so it was in his suffering, when God said, "My strength is made perfect in thy weakness."

Yet with all this hiding, there is one thing of the deepest possible moment, and that is, the reason why this thorn should be there. This the apostle cannot leave in the dark. He clearly feels that we ought all to know WHY the thorn came. It happened to him once, he says, to be just as happy as a man can be. It seems still, after fourteen years, that he was in heaven, whether in the body, or out of the body, he cannot tell. All he knows is, that these were the most exalted moments of his life; there he heard things he cannot report, because human language would fail to convey the idea if he were free to tell it, and right in the heart of that experience he got his thorn; it came then; it was there still; and the reason why it came is clear to him also. He was in danger of losing his balance, of being carried quite away by his felicity, and so losing the sense of his kinship to our pained and suffering humanity and his reliance upon Heaven, so there was given him a thorn in the flesh. And so it is when we know this much about the thorn, we can see that we do not need to know any more. The particular fact in the life of one man, opens thereby into an experience that is in some measure common to all. If we could know that Paul's thorn in the flesh was a defect in his eyes, or his speech, or a pain in his head, or the want of a foot to his stature, that particular thorn would fasten us down to a particular experience, and we should lose the great general lesson which I want to find, if I can, to-day, in speaking to you.

First, of the thorn in the flesh of our common humanity.

Second, what we can ourselves do about it. And,

Third, what can come to us with any thorn, if we can find out Paul's way of dealing with it.

And first, is it not true in a great general sense, that we all have some time a thorn in the flesh. Something that we do not care to describe by particulars, any more than Paul did, and would never mention without grave reason, but there it is, as sure as we live, and as long as we live, touching us to the quick with its pain now and then, and never letting us go quite so free as we were before it first began to stab us.

In the ranges of our common human history, we cannot fail to see the presence of this thorn in the greatest and noblest lives. Sometimes it is one thing, sometimes another. Now on the surface, and now in the nature. Those that soar highest, as Paul soared when he saw heaven, bear it with them, or bring it back, and carry it, as we do, wherever they go. It may be a mean thing, like Byron's club-foot; it shall torment me for all that, as if there is no greater misfortune possible to man than to go halting all his days; or it may be as great a thing as Dante's worship of Beatrice, as he appears in the picture, with that face, sad beyond expression, looking up to the beautiful saint, whose "soul was like a star, and dwelt apart,"— it shall be a thorn all the same to each man. Or it may be a great vice, like that which seized and held Coleridge and De Quincey, and put them down in the dungeon of the Giant Despair. Or it may be only like the dyspepsia, that now, in these days, darkens the whole vision of Mr. Carlyle, turning his beautiful afternoon into a grim and lurid sunset. But it is a thorn all the same, to all alike. In king David it was a great sin he never could forget if he lived to be as old as Methuselah, that stabbed him in his sons when penitence and God's grace had plucked it out of his soul. In Peter it was the memory of that morning, I suppose, when he cursed and swore, and turned his back on the noblest friend that ever a man had. In Luther it was a blackness of darkness that would come when it was ready, defying both physicians and philosophy, and beating down the soaring soul as a great hailstone beats down a bird. In Wesley it was a home without love, and a wife insane with jealousy, with an old love hidden away in his heart that was never permitted to bloom in his life, and so on through all the tale. Paul has no singularity: we need not be anxious about his mystery. Some of these things hurt him, and made the poor manhood of him quiver. The thorn in the flesh among the great ones of the world is a common possession. I said to a gentleman once, who told me he had been very intimate indeed with a great man, how was it that he should have fallen into such evil habits in his later life. "I must not tell you that," he said, "but I may tell you this, that he took to wine as a refuge from what to him seemed worse, at last, than drinking. It was pitiful it should be so, and he should do so; but knowing him as I do, I have always felt that my pity for him in these things should outreach my condemnation." It was Paul's delicate and shrouded way of saying it is a thorn in the flesh; but I will not tell you what it is. I was talking once again with a gentleman who knows very intimately one of our greatest living Americans, a man whose name will stand high in our history; and speaking especially of the felicity of the good providences that have attended him, I said he must be one of the happiest of men. "There is that in his life," my friend said, "you do not see, and very few are aware of. I knew him a long time before I guessed it: it is a pain that he carries about with him like his shadow; not a bodily, but a mental pain, which he will carry with him to his grave."

And so it is with us all — what the thorn is to these men in their great estate it may be to us in ours. It is true we can all see here and there a kindly, easy soul, which seems never to have felt the thorn, one which has certainly never soared as Paul had when he caught it, — whose temperament will make it hard, one thinks, for even Providence to find the nerve. I am not sure such a nature may not be thorn proof: I think sometimes it is. They say some fishes will go on feeding after what seem to be the most frightful inflictions, and evidently feel no pain. I have thought there might possibly be such a temperament as that among men. I remember in one of our Love Feasts in the Methodist church in England, thirty years ago and more, a man got up and told us how he had lost his wife by the fever, and then, one by one, all his children, and had felt as calm and serene through it as if nothing had happened; not suffering in the least; not feeling a pang of pain; fended and shielded, as he believed, by the Divine grace, and up to that moment, when he was talking to us, without a grief in his heart. As soon as he had done, the wise and manful old preacher who was leading the meeting got up, and said, " Now, brother, you go home, and into your closet, and down on your knees, and never get up again, if you can help it, until you are a new man.

What you have told us is not a sign of grace, it is a sign of the hardest heart I ever encountered in a Christian man. Instead of your being a saint, you are hardly good enough for a decent sinner. Religion never takes the humanity out of a man, it makes him more human; and if you were human at all, such trouble as you have had, ought to have broken your heart. I know it would mine, and I pretend to be no more of a saint than other people; so I warn you, never tell such a story as that in a Love Feast again."

That man was an instance of the sort of man who may have no thorn in the flesh. The old preacher saw it was not in the riches of God's grace, but in the poverty of his own nature, that he found his impunity from pain; and such impunity is possible to such men always; yet only as it is possible to fishes. But the law of life is to feel the thorn: the balance scale of ecstasy is agony. Poor Little Boston, in the exquisite story, still wanted to be buried in a grave six feet long. I never blamed Byron for feeling as he did about his foot; he could no more help that, with his nature, than he could help his lameness. The blame lay in his never summoning that strength to the maimed part, by which in his soul he could have outsoared the eagle, and outrun the deer, — the strength that is made perfect in our weakness.

And if I did not know that there is such a feeling abiding in some natures like a perpetual pain, I would not mention this in speaking especially of some thorns that can torment us. Certainly we do feel the pain of personal defect, and very naturally, because the standard of physical beauty and perfection is a thing civilized, and sensible men can no more alter than they can alter the standard of geometry. It was beautifully right in that old Mosaic religion which worshipped only Law, to enact that all offerings made to God should be physically perfect. The Lawgiver wanted to touch in this way the truth of physical perfection. It was wise and good, too, as far as it went, that the old Greek should so carefully keep the ideal beauty he dreamed of as the perfection of humanity actually embodied in marble and bronze before the eyes of his race. I have heard it doubted whether the mother sees what we see when one of her children fails of this standard. I know you can never guess she does from any word that falls from her lips; but she reveals her sense of it all the same, as the angels would reveal it, if such a thing as this imperfection were possible in heaven, by a brooding, watchful tenderness which knows no measure; which will guard and keep from the child itself the sense of the absent gift, while it magnifies immeasurably the gifts that are there. There is such a sense of what is fair and true in the outward appearance always in the common heart, that if we did not know this, we could still guess it, as we see the *ceaseless efforts which are made to hide what are thought to be defects, as well as to create what are thought to be beauties, but are often blank deformities, like that mincing fall from the line of uprightness, just now the fashion among women. We admire and value physical perfection. We notice and pity defects, or laugh at them if we have a bad heart. There are those who have to endure them, to whom they are a thorn in the flesh, bringing keen suffering sometimes, always casting something of a shadow, and begetting a morbid brooding in some natures far worse than they themselves can ever be. A feeling of bitterness, a sense of unfairness, and a wish that everything else in life could be bartered for this one thing, — perfection of the form or face.

Then, again, Paul's thorn in the flesh may have been a defect in his utterance. I can see what a thorn it is to many, that they can never adequately express their thought. They hear men talk, as oil runs, word slipping after word, without break or end, until the vessel is exhausted; or read essays and histories, in which the words fall into their place like music; but in the orator or the writer, they can see well enough that the thought bears no sort of proportion to the expression, while they feel they have something to say which would weigh with thinkers if they could only once get it out of its matrix; but it is like a diamond away down among the sunless pillars of the world, and there it is likely to stay. "You will find him to be a great lumbering wagon, loaded with ingots of gold," Robert Hall said of John Foster, when some congregation wrote to him and wanted to know whether Foster would do for a minister for their church, "and I hope you know gold when you see it, or else he will never do for you." They called him, and he failed, as he had failed in Dublin and Newcastle, and I do not know where besides. "Brother Foster," William Jay of Bath said to him once, "why don't you come and preach in my pulpit? I have been after you for years; my people want to hear you very much; now, why don't you come?" "Brother Jay," Foster said, "I love to feel there is one pulpit in England in which I can preach still, — it is yours. Now, if I preach only once for *you*, as you want me, I shall not have a pulpit. I mean to hold on to my one chance." But we possess two volumes of lectures by John Foster, that are among the grandest things of their sort in existence. They were born, as he tells us, with a sore travail, and given to a handful of people. He stands for my thought of this thorn in the flesh, that is just a dull aching to get expression for what is in the mind. Great numbers have it, in one way and another. It might not seem so from the deluge of words that is swamping church and commonwealth together; but it is so; and "I am slow of speech," is a very sad cry, as you hear it from such a man as first said it.

Nothing but Paul's saintliness again, and sure footing in dangerous places, has saved him from the guess that his thorn in the flesh was some sort of a bad passion or appetite. Very sore is this pain, and very common, and by no means so criminal as we sometimes think it is. In the far-reaching influences that go to every life, and away backward, as certainly as away forward, children are sometimes born with appetites fatally strong in their nature. As they grow up, the appetite grows with them, and speedily becomes a passion, the passion a master, the master a tyrant, and by the time he arrives at his manhood the man is a slave. There is no doctrine that demands a larger vision than this of the depravity of human nature. I believe, in the judgment-day, which comes at last to every soul, two men may stand before the great white throne together, one with a great many bad things to answer for, and the other with very few; yet the one who appears to be the greater criminal, shall be deemed the better man; because he has fought his battle at a vast disadvantage, while the other has had everything in his favor. The worse man, as we have to call him, found when he got fairly into life, that these appetites and passions would rage, and tear, and trample over him, and had to be mastered at last by endeavors which would have saved ten men no worse tempted than the one who stands beside him. "Why don't you make an effort and put your passion down, once for all," a good friend of mine, a preacher, said to one of these poor sinners. "Doctor," he replied, "I've tried more, and harder, I believe, than you need try twenty times over, and I am nothing but an old sinner still." You see it is like two men coming of age, and getting each one a farm, and going to work to raise a crop. The one farm is fair and sweet, has been watched and tended and kept in good order; the other is as full of weeds and briers as a place can be, with all the fences down, and neglect wherever you turn. Now, what merit is there in the one man's keeping the good place good, in comparison with that by which the other has made the bad place better. Old Dr. Mason used to say, as much grace as would make John a saint, would barely keep Peter from knocking a man down. The appetite which has grown into a passion, that needs to be bitted and bridled, or guarded as you guard wild beasts within iron bars, is a thorn in the flesh, a dreadful sharp thorn, from which its possessor can never be free, as men are free who possess a nature full of fine balances; and to be a man at last under such disadvantages, not to mention a saint, is as fine a piece of grace as can well be seen. Everywhere about us there are those who feel this thorn. I heard a man say once, that for eight and twenty years the soul within him had to stand, like an unsleeping sentinel, guarding his appetite for strong drink.

And so I might go on to tell almost endlessly about these thorns in the flesh. With one man, it is every now and then a black day, like those that came to Luther; with another, it is the bitter memory of a great sin, or a great wrong, or a great mistake, which stays like a ghost, and cannot be laid. It is a pain in the citadel of life with another, that can never be removed, but will rack and wrench at its own will, in spite of all that the doctors can do. While with men like great Edward Irving, and Robert Hall, and Jonathan Swift, it is the fine edge, as sharp as that over which the Mussulman dreams he will pass into

Paradise, dividing the most transcendent genius from its saddest ruins.

Now, then, secondly, I was to ask what we can do about it. I say, we ourselves can do one of two very different things,— we can make the best of it, or the worst of it. And I do not mean just now what Paul did with his thorn when he went to the Infinite Mercy about it, but what we can do about ours, apart from the question of that Divine Power to help us, which I shall have to mention thirdly, as the most blessed thing of all. If I find myself, for instance, in early life in the possession of a passion that is rapidly growing into a curse, I can submit to its dictate without a struggle, as I see some do, can give in to its fascination with a shameful subservience, I can let it drag me down into its caves and devour me alive, or I can stand up and fight it; I do not say conquer, I say fight with all the might there is in me; fight for my life as I would fight for my home, and my wife and children, or anything that is supremely worth fighting for; because I take it, that apart from God's grace, there is a certain manliness possible to every man who is still in any sense in possession of himself.

I notice the police in London have lately asserted they never feel in any danger from the secret malice of the London thieves, no matter how often they may have brought them into trouble, if, as they say, they have been on the square with them, told the exact truth about their rogueries, and shown them such fair play as even a rogue thinks he has a right to. It shows how even in that utterly lost life, one little spot is still clear for the growth of some poor spark of manliness, that shall maintain the difference between the truth and the lie, while yet the living depends upon perpetual falsehood. It is hard to imagine again, any man, as a rule, more empty of what we would call Religion, than the common soldier. His whole life, poor fellow, makes it very hard for him to have any sense of it, and he has very little. But it has come out since the great Sepoy rebellion in India, that numbers of these men in the English army were offered the alternative of renouncing the Christian religion and embracing that of the rebels, or being murdered by all the horrible ways the hate and rage of the pagans could invent. It is believed that they died to a man: not one instance as yet has come to light of any common soldier giving way. He might not be a Christian, or have seen the inside of a church since he was carried there as a babe to be baptized. He might only use the name of him who died on the tree for blasphemy, and have no conception of the grace that abides forever at the heart of the holy church throughout all the world. But he was a man belonging on that side, and the pincers could not tear that simple manliness out of his heart, or the fire burn it out. He knew that his sisters and brothers sang the old hymns, and sent their children to the Sunday schools, and that the white-haired father and mother were at rest in the old churchyard. He knew no hymns, he had no children, he would be thrown to the tigers in the jungle what time his soul had gone out on its doleful way; but he was a man of that stock. He might meet them again. He would tell them, if he did, that he died with the Cross in his eyes and not the Crescent, and so he went to his doom. And so there may be manliness where there is little grace, if by grace you mean that gracious thing, a pure and holy life and a conscious religion. It is all I plead for in this second thought. I may have the thorn in my flesh of a personal blemish. I can bear it like a man, manfully and modestly, until it almost shines with beauty. I may be always aware of my painful unreadiness and inability to be what my nature assures me I might be. I can be so manly in bearing my burden that my silence shall be golden. I may find myself in possession of an enemy within my nature, more dangerous than the whole banded might of the world. I stand for something still; I do not belong on that side; I belong to the banner of the cross: a voice in my soul whispers, "Son of man, stand upon thy feet!" "Did I break down? was I unmanned?" one of the great men I have mentioned said, when the thorn in the flesh had hurt him so terribly that he lost his consciousness. He felt he must be a man even then. Indeed, I know no one condition of life in which the thorn can pierce us, which can reveal a more beautiful manliness or womanliness than our quietness through intense physical, or mental, or spiritual pain. To be steady then, is to be steady indeed. I bow before such valor with a bare head. To see the patient face on which pain has graven its lines, reflecting an unconquered soul, is to be aware of a royalty to which the purple robe and acclamation are a vain show.

I said, thirdly, we must see what can come of the thorn in the flesh, if we find out Paul's way of dealing with it.

From what he feels it clearly appears he can tell us about his own particular case, that he tried the best he knew; bore his trouble man fashion, as well as he could; but then found he was still unable to win much of a victory. The pain was there still, and perhaps the shame of it, and he felt as if he would have to give way at last, and go down, as Christian did when he was fighting Apollyon. So, in the simple old fashion, he took the matter into the Supreme Court, and said, "I want this thorn removed: I can bear it no longer. I am sick of trying to get along with it." But the Judge said, "No, it must stay: that is in the nature of things, and cannot be altered. To take it away would be to destroy the grace to which it points. I will not take the bane, but I will give you another blessing."

Lately, when I crossed Suspension Bridge, I

got talking with a gentleman about the crystallization of iron. We agreed that every train which crossed the bridge did something to disintegrate the iron particles and break the bridge down. It was clear to us both, that if this process could go on long enough, there would be a last train, which would shoot right down into the green, boiling gulf, with all the horrors of the terrible catastrophe. But we concluded this would probably never come to pass, because we are finding out how long it takes to crystallize a piece of iron; and so, before there is any great danger, all these strands and cables will be made over again in the fire and under the hammer, and come out as strong and good as ever; so the fire and hammer, in such a case, would be in themselves the best blessing that can come to these ever-weakening strands. Nothing else could do them any good. To take them out, put others in, and then let these lie at rest on the banks of the Niagara, would be no sort of use. The iron-masters would laugh at you for doing that. They would say, "That will do more harm than good; it will make the strands eternally unfit for their purpose: only the hammer and fire can make them very good, and these can make them better and stronger than ever." Is not this also the law of life, that the fineness and strength essential to our best being, and to make us do our best work, come by the hammer and the fire? by the thorn in the flesh, the trouble and pain in our life, which may act in us as the fire acts in the iron, welding the fibre afresh, and creating the whole anew (as the Apostle would say) unto good works? We go along in our easy way, with nothing in particular to do or bear beyond ordinary duties and burdens; and then there is nothing particular in our nature. But suddenly some great trouble comes, — some thorn in the flesh, — and breaks up the old monotony. The good time, in that sense, is over; and then, though we may feel sore, and savage about it, towards the Providence that is above us, we are drawn towards those nearest to us with a new tenderness and trust. The strands that bind us are better; we are better men and women. I dare trust the worst brute in this city to be good to his wife, if he has helped to nurse the buried babe she is breaking her heart about. The thorn, for the time he feels it, has made a man of him. And so we touch, right here, the element in the strength that Paul had, while he had the thorn. The trouble itself, whatever it was, held the new power. He found it was as much more to his life, as Calvary is more than Canaan to the life of the world, and then he gave up all idea of getting rid of the thorn. So, as we can see that not the weddings, but the crucifixions, are the mighty things of history; not the festivals, but the battles; not the ovations, but the martyrdoms,—we find the first grace that can come from Heaven to help us bear our thorn in the flesh, whatever it be, — a personal misfortune; inability to be all that we feel we ought to be; the possession of a passion we have to watch with unslumbering care; pain that defies all doctors; darkness of the spirit, against which there is no argument; the sore of a bitter old sin; a home in which there is no light of a true love; a great and incurable disappointment; or the death of our brightest and best — I say these may be the very conditions of the grace which is made "perfect in our weakness." Joyfulness has its own place; gladness is the wine of life; but the life-blood comes of the struggle, and the Saviour is the Man of Sorrows. Yet we can never be sure of this as we should be, until the great thing Paul had, to make the best of his thorn, is ours also, and that is, the uplifting and out-going of the heart to God. The out-going of the heart in faith, and prayer, and patience; and the confidence, that while I rest in the sense of my Father's wisdom and love, and do the best I can, things will be just about what they should be, and would be, if I were the sole being besides the Father in the universe, and he had no thought but to make everything come into harmony with my desire. It is always the old history over again we have to realize, before we can be entirely at rest. The cup is held to our lips, and we shrink back, and cry, "Let this pass from me;" but then the soul says, "The cup that *my* Father has given me, shall I not drink it?" and we say, "Thy will be done," and then there is quiet. The sun shines in the soul then, though it is black night outside; and though we have to bear after that the kiss of the traitor, and the curse of the fiend, and the crown of thorns, all in the flesh together, and the cross and shame, we can bear all, and be all, while we rest in God, and look up to our great Forerunner, whose life, from the time he came forth to help us bear our burdens was one long pain, the thorn always hurting; that so we might learn how the way to the loftiest life in heaven may lie through the roughest ways of earth.

> " 'Tis alone of His appointing
>   That our feet on thorns have trod;
> Suffering, pain, renunciation,
>   Only bring us nearer God.
>
> " Strength sublime may rise from weakness,
>   Groans be turned to songs of praise;
> Nor are life's divinest labors
>   Only told by songs of praise."

III.

EVERY MAN A PENNY.

Matthew xx. 9: "He gave every man a penny."

I suppose we have all noticed the curious diversity of the seeds we sow in the spring. There are some that shoot out and grow up days before the others from the same paper, sown in the same bed, and that seemed exactly like the rest. It is so with a number of fruit trees in a young orchard. Each tree may get an equal care, and appear to have the same natural advantages, but one will spring out into an early fruitfulness, while another holds back, summer after summer, and perhaps, only when the husbandman begins to despair of its ever doing any good, it bears fruit.

It is so with boys. One lad will be bright and promising, the joy of his tutor, and the pride of his mother, right from the start; no one can tell exactly how he learned his letters; they seemed to come to him by instinct; he knew them when he saw them, or, as Plato would say, he re-collected them. But another lad, on the same form, perhaps in the same family, is dull and backward; he has quite forgotten his first letters before he learned the last. But after a good while there is the dawn of a new day; then the backward boy has a whole sunrise to himself, and opens out into an equal manhood with the best of his brighter fellows.

It is so again with woman in the experiences and life of the heart. A shrinking, retiring, near-sighted woman waits and waits among the Yorkshire hills, saying, wistfully, to herself, "What shall I do?" It has been a long, sore trial to wait and watch as she has done. In her lifetime she has known not a few of her own age who have long since solved that problem: some are wedded and happy in their homes; others have found their true place as teachers, writers, or artists, and are crowned already with honor. This woman has had great sorrows, and sore losses, and her day is wearing on into the afternoon, still she has heard no voice bidding her go work in the vineyard. There is a letter written to Wordsworth while she stands there in the market-place waiting for the Master, that is, in my opinion, the most pathetic cry ever heard in our lifetime. " Sir," she says, " I earnestly entreat you to read and judge what I have sent you. From the day of my birth to this day I have lived in seclusion here among the hills, where I could neither know what I was nor what I could do. I have read, for the reason that I have eaten bread, because it was a real craving of nature, and have written on the same principle. But now I have arrived at an age when I must do something. The powers I possess must be used to a certain end; and as I do not know them myself, I must ask others what they are worth: there is no one here to tell me if they are worthy; and if they are worthless, there is no one to tell me that. I beseech you to help me." What she sends to Wordsworth then, is poor; she has written many volumes, all poor; has waited in the market-place and done no work; but at last, the Master, walking there, sees her wistful face turned towards him, and says, " Go into my vineyard." Then she bends over some small folded sheets of coarse paper until her face almost touches them, and in one book she storms the heart of England and America, and in the one hour that was left her she won her penny.

Another woman sits in her room in pleasant old Canterbury; her life has been lonely also, and she says to herself, "What shall I do?" She feels about and finds a pen, and it is not hard to see that there is a gift of God in the things she is doing long before she takes her great place; still it is only waiting. The Master comes, and the voice says, "Go work in my vineyard." Then, as she wiles us with the story of a woman, who was a Methodist and a preacher, and tells of the fortunes of those who were subject to her irresistible sway, she opens such hidden wells of tender truth and goodness, and dear homely humanity, as this world hardly believed could be treasured in its heart in these latter days; and now in other books following that, she has gone into the first rank of those that work for God in that corner of his vineyard, and has won her penny.

It is so again in the world of men. One man starts ahead, and distances all about him; he will never have an equal, is the verdict of the world; another, of the same age, stands where he was placed. At last something stirs him, and he starts too; and while the first man never stops, the last comes up and runs abreast, or goes ahead. Charles Dickens sits in his chambers in London in the full fame of his Pickwick Papers. He is preparing a new book, to be brought out as that was, with illustrations. A man comes in, older than himself, but still a young man, and says, "I have come, sir, to show you some drawings, and to get the place, if I can, of artist for your new story." The young author glances over the sketches, and then says, kindly, "They will not do." The man goes home, puts aside his pencil, partially, and takes a pen. He works for years after this, writing small books and pieces for magazines, but wins no notice, and is almost altogether unknown. One day, however, he goes to a bookseller in London with a new work, asks him to print it, and fails to persuade him. Another agrees to do it, with fear of the result; but when the book is printed, the most popular writer in Britain has, from that day, a divided kingdom. And when this man died, suddenly, some years ago, tens of thousands, who had never seen his face, mourned for him as for a dear friend; and now vast numbers, of the truest insight, will tell you that the poor artist, whose work was kindly refused, was the first man of his age in the department of letters, in which he once would have been glad and proud to be a servant of one of the servants of the Master who hires and pays us all.

It is so again in our practical common life. One man begins early, and is a notable man from the start. He goes on in his career, gathering honor and success; the common heart is in his hand; when he speaks all listen; when he writes all read. Another works hard on a frontier farm, or teaches a country school, or tries a flat-boat on the river, feeling dimly all the while that this is only waiting; the time has not come for him to enter the vineyard. But at last, as he stands watching and waiting, the voice says, "Go thou also;" and presently those who have been the longest at work feel that he will win his penny. He had but one or two hours; he suffers no loss; he stands, at last, abreast of the very foremost of all.

This is true again of the spiritual life. The old prophet kept his flock, or followed his plough; and the old scholar drank at all the fountains of wisdom and inspiration. Josephus and Philo are masters in the highest attainments of their age; John and Peter are peasants and fishermen; Paschal and Jeremy Taylor seem as if they were born for the sacred robes, so early and so beautifully do they wear them; John Bunyan is, to all seeming, a born tinker, and George Fox a born cobbler. So there is for them a long waiting and watching, and the cry, " What shall I do? " At last the voice says, " Go thou also." Then the grace and glory of the vines they have tended are a world's wonder, and their fruit a world's blessing.

This is true, finally, of our country. England and Germany begin in the early morning, and in the wild woods of Britain and Gaul, to earn their penny; and it is their lot for long centuries to toil, winning, as they can, this and that from the wilderness,— trial by jury, Magna Charta, free speech, free press, free pulpit,— and when many hours are past, and much hard work is done, a voice comes to a new nation, and tells of a new world, and says, " Go work there ; " and when the old world looks up, the new is abreast of those nations that have borne the burden and heat of the day, and will have its penny. And in this new world itself, there are men living here in Chicago, who can remember very well when our great prairies lifted their faces wistfully to the sun, and cried, "No man hath hired us;" when our streets, now so full of life, sounded only to the voice of the mighty waters and the cry of the savage. Now the whole civilized world has to come and see what has been done. Not many years more will pass, we who live here believe, before this new worker will be abreast of the oldest, and will win her penny. For so God comes and goes: selecting, calling, and settling all things according to the counsel of his own will. No man can stay his hand, or say, What doest thou? He sitteth in the heavens, and his kingdom is in all the earth. "For the kingdom of heaven is like unto a man that is a householder, which went out early in the morning, and at the third hour, and at the sixth, and at the ninth, and at the eleventh hour, and hired laborers for a penny a day. So when the even was come, the Lord said, Call the laborers, and give them their hire, beginning from the first even unto the last. And they that came first, and they that came last, received every man his penny."

The parable is said to be meant for a lesson to the Jews at the moment when God was about to call the Gentiles into his vineyard also, and give them a place they had never filled before in working out his will. It is possible this meaning may lie within the parable in some remote way; but I cannot believe that this is all the Saviour meant when he spoke to the Jews. The truth is, that then as now, and forever, there are great numbers of men and women waiting in the market-place, in all sorts of ways, watching for the coming of the Master to set them to work; to give them their true place in this life; the place they know they can fill — men and women who have never found their calling, and yet have never ceased to watch for it, and wait with weary, hungry, patient eyes, and to say, "What shall I do?" We look at them, very likely, as we stand in our place doing our work, and despise them for what we call their shiftlessness; when if we did but know the whole truth, we might wonder over them for their power to do what is harder than any hard work ever could be to such natures,— to wait for work, such as they ought to do, and hear no command to go. These were in the world then as they are now, and this Divine soul, which saw everything that had a sorrow in it, saw them; and the heart that had a sympathy, sweet and abundant as a full honeycomb, took them all in, and then cried to the Father to know the truth about this; and the truth came in this parable of those that work, and those that wait; touching with its consolation the waiters, too; giving them their place in life and their promise; and bidding the worker pause in his hasty judgment of those who wait until he is quite sure that the waiter is not the most worthy of the two.

For this, I think, must be clear, first of all, as we study this mystery of waiters and workers, there can be no pleasure in waiting, in standing all the day idle, and looking wistfully, as the hours pass by, for some one to hire us, feeling the beat and tingle in nerve and brain that would gladly find some worthy task where nothing worthy comes. It is not the young man whose whole career is a constant success, or the young woman who finds her home or her place at once in life; not these the tender intention of the parable touches first and last: it is the young man who has to stand back, and notice painfully how he is distanced by his fortunate or clever companions who go right on; and the woman, whose hair, by and by, begins to show threads of silver while she is compelled to look wistfully and wofully into the silent heavens, into the deeps of our human life, everywhere watching for the coming of the Lord, who shall tell her what to do. Yet the day wears on, and she cries, as one hour strikes after another, "Woe is me! What shall I do?" It is the man who is dimly conscious of power and purpose somewhere within his soul, yet is compelled, year after year, to toil on twenty acres of hard-scrabble, or push a flat-boat, or teach a district school and board round, aware all the time that this is only waiting for the coming of the Lord, — yet to wait, and watch, and hear no voice. It is into these wistful eyes the compassionate Christ looks as he speaks his parable, and not into ours, who are working where we want to be, and feel sure of our wages.

And this, if I understand the parable, is the first consolation we touch in it, and good for all time. The ultimate reason why some have to stand and wait, who sorely want to work, rests not with us at all, but with the Lord, who calls us when he will, and gives us our reward; not merely for working faithfully, but for waiting faithfully as well. It shows us that away down within this want of power to see and do, we are to believe in the will of God concerning us. So that what we see in such lives as I have touched, for example, we must see in the life of every worthy man and woman who has to wait and watch; who tries and fails, and has to stand back, God knows why, we say in our pride, and they in their patience. We are both right; God does know why; and that is the most intimate reason. He has determined it shall be so, that his purpose may be answered in that one life, and in the whole commonwealth of the world. As we seem to see the things through a glass darkly, when we notice how he kept North America waiting when China was called, and then kept the West waiting when the East was called; waiters and workers, — this has always been the Divine order. Lands, nations, providences, discoveries, the whole world, outside the personal life of the man and woman, are full of my parable.

So, then, when I see a young man slow and

backward, and in a poor place, whose soul I know would expand in the sunshine of prosperity and fill a better place; or a woman, waiting with her unfulfilled life in her heart, willing to give it in any high, pure fashion to the Lord, if he will but come and take it; or a preacher, with a mighty power to preach somewhere in his nature, if he could only find the clew to it; or a man who has waited through his lifetime for the Lord to show him the true church, the place where he can feel that the religious heart of him is at rest; — if in these things, or in any of them, I feel I have found my place, and am doing my work, I must feel very tenderly, and judge very generously, all the waiters in all these ways; must call up this picture of the faces so wistful in the old market-place, watching for the coming of the Lord : " Who has made me to differ, who has called me at the first hour, why do I succeed where others fail?" It is the gift of God; it is not of works, lest any man should boast. It is the difference between the seed the husbandman, for his own good reason, will leave dark and still in the granary, and the seed he sows which can spring at once to the sun and the sweet airs of summer. It is the difference in the home, in our conduct towards our children, when we know it is best to let one go forward in the school and keep another back; yet both decisions come out of our heart's best love, and are made through what we know, but the children do not know, of their present and future. So this working and waiting lies in the will of God, and God is my Father, and this is the predestination of my Father's love.

There is another thing in this parable we must not miss; I have touched it already, but not all it needs: it is the eager wistfulness and readiness in those faces of the waiters; the sure sign that when they are called, they will be ready to go. If they had been indifferent or asleep, the Master might have passed them by; if they had not been ready also in the sense of knowing what to do, they would have had only disgrace and no penny. The two great sources of failure, when the fault lies at all in ourselves, are to be found first, in not keeping our heart and life awake to the call of God, and, second, in not knowing how to take hold when we are called. Every man and woman who has achieved a real success in any way whatever, from the forging of a horse-shoe to the saving of a soul, succeeded through being ready when the call came. You believe that a lucky hit, as we call it, made them what they are. I tell you, Nay; whatever has come out of the head, and heart, and hand of any man or woman, first went into it in some quick, genuine, human fashion. They builded better than they knew, but they knew they builded: John Bunyan was the pilgrim who made the Progress; George Fox quaked and trembled, it was Wesley's methods that made the Methodist; and before the slaves could be free, Garrison must be bound with them. No man or woman ever won the penny by accident. If you will be sure that the longing you feel for something better is not to end in disgrace when your call comes, you must now be gathering the ideas and aptitudes that will insure the place; keep your whole life open and ready; then when the Master comes, and says, "That is the place you are to fill, and the work you are to do," you shall find that to you, as fully as to those that were called before you, comes the full reward.

There is one thing more; it has lurked in some

of your hearts and minds all the time I have been talking. You say you can tell me of men and women who never could do what they longed to do, but only had it in them to do it, and could never get it out; men and women as noble as those I have mentioned for illustration, and as good, but lonely and unknown to the last, and they died hearing no call from the Master, but only waiting until the sun set and they went home. Yes, and I myself have known such men and women, whose lot, from the place where I stood looking at it, seemed as sad as a tragedy; and yet this was the wonder of it, that somehow they themselves were generally among the most cheerful and happy people at last under the great canopy of heaven. For one thing they generally do get a poor little show of some sort before they get through, and it does them more good than we can tell. It does not take much coin to come to a penny, but a penny to them has a wonderful worth; they feel somehow, at last, as a rule, with very few exceptions, that, taken altogether, their lines have fallen in pleasant places. And then standing there, watching and waiting, there have come to them a patience and power that seldom come to the prosperous and happy — to those that have everything they want.

I think the most heart-whole man I ever knew, was a man who had waited and watched, breaking stones through all weathers on the cold shoulder of a Yorkshire hill, and he could hardly see the stones he had to break he was so sand blind. His wife was dead and all his children; his hut was open to the sky, and to the steel-cold stars in winter; but when once one said, to comfort him, "Brother, you will soon be in heaven!" he cried out in his rapture, "I have been there this ten years!" And so when at last the angel came to take him, he was not unclothed, but clothed upon; mortality was swallowed up of life.

I treasure a small drawing by Millais. It is the figure of a woman bound fast to a pillar far within tide mark. The sea is curling its tides about her feet; a ship is passing in full sail, but not heeding her or her doom; birds of prey are hovering about her, but she heeds not the birds, or the ship, or the sea; her eyes look right on, and her feet stand firm, and you see that she is looking directly into heaven, and telling her soul how the sufferings of this present time are not worthy to be compared with the glory that shall be revealed; and under the picture is this legend, copied from the stone set up to her memory in an old Scottish kirkyard:—

> "Murdered for owning Christ supreme,
> Head of His Church, and no more crime.
> But for not owning prelacy,
> And not abjuring presbytery,
> Within the sea, tied to a stake,
> She suffered for Christ Jesus' sake."

I treasure it, because when I look at it, it seems a type of a great host of women who watch and wait, tied fast to their fate, while the tide creeps up about them, but who rise as the waves rise, and on the crest of the last and loftiest are borne into the quiet haven, and hear the "Well-done!"

IV.

THE TWO HARVESTS.

Rom. vii. 4: "Fruit unto God."

It has come to me, now that the last fruits of the year are being gathered, to say something to you of the lesson that lies within our harvest, touching the harvest of life. And I want to speak of it in the light of the suggestion that rises naturally out of my text, and try, if I can, to find what is fruit unto God. What is fruit to us, is a question not very hard to answer; but fruit to God, I propose to show, is unspeakably more, look at it as we will, than what is fruit to us.

And in doing this, I shall speak to you, —

I. Of the vastness of his harvest compared with ours.

II. Of its variety, and

III. Of its ripening.

First, then, we have to notice the difference

every harvest-time brings home to us between our conception and that of the Divine Providence, of what is really good fruit in the measure of it. It is at once quite evident, when we begin to look into it, that the gift of God in the harvest he ripens is so great, it can only be held in his own measure. We see it is not merely this granary of ours that is full; there is another granary besides this, in which a harvest is stored of seed for sowing, and bread for eating, to which this of ours is a mere handful, and all this is as good in its way, as the fruit and corn on which we have come to set such store. There are seeds so small that the human eye cannot see them, and fruits of the wilderness so manifold, as to far exceed, as yet, our power to find them out: they are scattered through all the zones of the world, from the Iceland moss in the Arctic circle to the palm-tree under the line. The whole world outside our little storehouse is one great granary, " a house not made with hands," in which things are laid up that are good, in one way or another, for all the families in the many mansions of the Maker and Provider, from whose full hand we are all fed. Our good fruit in this light is one thing, his good fruit another; and so, as the heavens are higher than the earth, his thought of what is good must be higher than our own.

Whatever we may think of the thorns and thistles that came up outside Eden to curse the land, what he said was good, when he made the earth bring forth grass, and the herb yielding seed, and the fruit-trees yielding fruit after their kind, is good still; there has been no debasement of this Divine husbandry; no empty granary of God; no failure of the field. He tills for the multitude that cry to him for bread. I look up, at the end of the harvest that he has gathered, and the wonder and joy of it seem to me unspeakable. He crowns the year with his goodness to every living thing.

This is true again, when we turn from the vastness of this treasure to its variety. We get some sense of this from what we agree to call good fruit. We see how the corn differs from the apple, and the grape from the chestnut; how the plum can never be like the melon, or the walnut as the blackberry; and in this variety there is a blessing that could never be found, if the best of all the things God has given us could have been selected for our sole use, and poured out upon us from his hand in the full measure of our wishes.

So I cannot find in my heart to condemn Israel for crying out against the manna, good as it seems to have been, and full of nourishment, when they found that was all they had; and then that they should look back longingly to Egypt, by and by, and hanker after the cucumbers and melons, the variety of the good fruit they had left in the old country; and then when quails came, that they should devour them with such eagerness as to bring on a plague.

I do not find that with the heavenly manna there was any alteration in the human appetite: that remained as it always had been; it remained, therefore, to torment them; it was not in their human nature to be content with angels' food, so long as they were still in the flesh. And I have no idea of what was grown in Eden; but I know that if Eden did not grow such a variety in its harvests as this that now blesses all civilized men, it was not so good a place to live in, in some respects, as this city, and would not be so likely to satisfy the whole demand of our life. Let this be as it may, the variety that we ourselves take note of, is as divine as the abundance. Yet it is but a fragment of the whole variety that is harvested in the garners of God. We are constantly coming into possession of some new fruit or seed that brings a new blessing; but beyond that, other races have their blessings, differing from ours, specially adapted to their sustenance and joy. And then there is a vast store of things that ripen every harvest, we know very little about, or take to be worthless, but in their own place and for their own purpose they are all good fruits. The variety in the harvest that God reaps is as wonderful as the vastness.

So it is again when we turn from the harvest to the harvest-time. We naturally think of what is gathered now, and laid up for the bleak days that are coming. But the truth is, ever since the snow-drop came up through the snow, and blessed us in the wild, spring weather, there has been a perpetual ingathering of ripe things. The spring blossoms ripened when our eyes had been gladdened, and our hearts had fed on their beauty and sweetness, and when their time came they passed away; they are harvested in the granaries of life; the corruptible has put on incorruption, and the mortal, immortality; they are not in our memory merely, but in our being.

The first fruits of summer came: it was ordained of Heaven that they should not wait for the later harvest; they must ripen in June, or not at all; and so they ripened and were gathered, and reckoned in the harvest of the year. There were other fruits that came to their perfection in the strong sun of August. They must be gathered when they were ripe: they could not wait for the early frosts; and they are a part of the harvest too, just as truly as the grapes and corn. The completeness of harvest, then, is in the great span of it; and we only understand the whole truth of what is fruit unto God, when we understand and feel how good it is for our life to take in this long ripening, together with the vastness and variety. No human eye may ever see myriads of blessings we must count in the harvest of God, and yet the blue-bell, waving in the wilderness, shall be a sky of azure fretted with gold for a host of God's creatures living under its vast dome and rejoicing in the completeness of its blessing.

This, then, is the truth about the harvest we are completing. We have one measure for it: He who clothes the lilies and feeds the birds has another. We gather a few varieties; he bids nature and his angels gather all. We think of this as the harvest-time: harvest began when we felt the breath of the first snowdrop, and blessed it for heralding the glory of the year; and this is the truth that fills the soul fullest of the goodness of God. The more completely we can grasp the vastness, the variety, and the long ripening of the harvest, the more deeply we can feel the presence of his providence and grace.

I said the harvest of the year leads us on to the harvest of life; the vastness, and variety, and difference in the ripening of humanity, and the difference between our estimate of it and the estimate of Heaven. In my boyhood, when I listened to sermons, and through some years of the time I preached them, my idea of the harvest of Humanity, and what is good fruit to God, was very simple. A long, narrow strip in the great wilderness of the world bore good fruit, all the rest was left to grow things whose end is to rot, or to be burned. That was the way I was taught to believe in the harvest of Humanity, — the good fruit that the angels gathered; and, God forgive me, it was the way I tried to teach others. Adam, Seth, Enoch, Methuselah, Lamech, Noah, Shem, and so down to Abraham and Lot, with a patch somewhere on one side for Melchisedec; then by Joseph and Moses, and the Judges to David, and by the Prophets down to Christ; then from Christ, the narrow belt of the True Church in and out of the Church of Rome to the Reformation, and then through the Puritans, down to this age. That was the way we got at the harvest of Humanity; of what was especially worth garnering of all that grew in the wilderness of this world, for about six thousand years, as near as we could tell by Bishop Lowth's chronology.

It is by no means the exclusive task of liberal Christianity now to deny this wretched, narrow dogma; the best preachers of every faith in Christendom are proclaiming the truth, our preachers were among the first to proclaim from the pulpit, that fruit unto God is grown and gathered in every nation, and kindred, and people, and tongue. That Assyria, and Egypt, and Greece, and Rome, and Arabia, and Ethiopia, and Scandinavia, and old Gaul, bore their harvests as certainly as the Hebrew and Christian lands. That what the church and the preacher insisted on as the true harvest exclusively, is only the harvest of a few varieties, of which the noblest Christian fruit is no doubt the best of all, but that finds its full perfection too in what it draws from all the rest.

This is the truth of the vastness, and variety, and long ripening of the harvest of God in the whole human family. The field is the world; no narrow ribbon, but all the zones, from the equator to the poles. It is the grand verity that Paul caught out of heaven as he stood on Mars Hill, and cried, God made the world, and *all* things therein. He giveth to *all* life, and breath, and all things. He hath made of one blood all nations of men to dwell on all the face of the earth, and he is not far from every one of us — the children of Cain as well as of Seth, of Ishmael as well as Isaac, by the Iliads as surely as the Psalms, by Athens as by Jerusalem, by Pagan as by Christian Rome, and in Saracen as in Christian Spain. Everywhere the harvest of Humanity has ripened through its infinite variety, and from the spring-time of the world to the autumn.

We are gradually coming to the conviction again, that this is the truth about the divine ingathering to-day — what is fruit unto God, good men in all churches and out of them are saying, cannot be this small handful alone in the Christian garner. That is no doubt the best wherever it comes to its full perfection, but there is a divine reaping where the Christian seed was never sown. This old idea of an exclusive goodness and acceptance among Christians, is very much like what we see sometimes at our State fairs. Men come there who have set their hearts on some one thing, and given their life to its development. The consequence is, very naturally, that they cannot weigh the worth of quantities of good fruits and seeds which differ from theirs, or even from their special variety of the same thing, and have no faculty at all for estimating the good that is not good enough to be *shown*, but that lies in an infinite wealth in the world outside the Fair ground.

We have far too much of this in our churches

still. We devote ourselves to the cultivation of our variety, and train our vision away, through our devotion, from seeing, as we should, what worth there is in the varieties to which we have given no attention. If we allow these to be good again, but not so good as ours, we think little of the great harvest of good outside this wider circle. But there it is, filling the world with blessing. And so it is with the whole harvest of Humanity to-day. There is not a nation or people anywhere that is not, according to its variety, bringing forth fruit to God — something good answering to its condition, as truly as the harvests answer to the zones of the world. It is not our sort; perhaps we cannot see what use there is in it; it is not our business. What we have to do is to make the best of the corner of the vineyard the Master has given us, and then to believe that he will see to the rest, and will not let it run to waste. In China and India, as well as in America, the Lord of the harvest holds his own; for the field is the world, and the reapers are the angels; and in vastness, in variety, and in the span of the harvest, it is the same yesterday, to-day, and forever.

This brings me to say again, that the same thing comes home to us about the life that is close to ours. What I have said about Christian ideas of the multitudes of heathens all the world over, I must insist on in connection with those in our own land, who are not Christians, and never will be. I can no more believe that the mere handful of our countrymen who are gathered into churches are all that are going to be gathered into heaven, than that the barns and cellars of the country hold all the good that has ripened this fall. I am the last man, I trust, to say a word that shall seem to make the Christian faith and the Christian church anything else but what it is. What I will say is this, that the religious life is by no means confined to the Christian faith and churches. There is a very great deal we never think of calling religion, that is still fruit unto God, and garnered by Him in the harvest. The fruits of the Spirit are love, joy, peace, long suffering, gentleness, patience, goodness. I affirm, that if these fruits are found in any form, they are the fruits of the Spirit, whether you show your patience as a woman nursing a fretful child, or as a man attending to the vexing detail of a business, or as a physician following the dark mazes of sickness, or as a mechanic fitting the joints and valves of a locomotive; being honest, and true besides, you bring forth fruit unto God.

I went into a picture-store one day, and met a lady, who said, " Come and look at a picture." I suppose you have most of you seen it. There are two figures in it; one is a soldier — one of our own — wounded and sick, worn and weary, with a white face, and great, out-looking eyes, that seem as if they were watching for the chariot of heaven. The other is a Sister of Mercy, with a book in her hand, reading. She has one of those sweet, clear faces we all remember, in which no trace of human passion glasses itself any more, but only the quietness and assurance of a heart at rest.

"What do you think of it?" my friend said. I expressed my sense of its beauty; but then I had to tell her how sure I was that it was not the Sister, with her prayer-book, that stood for the pure, religious devotion of that scene; the poor fellow there, almost dead, was, to me, the most religious of the two. I could not look behind him, as I could behind the woman, through long years of fasting, and prayer, and aspiration. That might be there, or it might not; the probabilities were against it; but what was there that I could see, was a love that could make the man leap out of his home to the front; a joy that he could make his breast a barrier for the motherland; peace in duty well done; long suffering in the doing, down to that moment; and gentleness, and patience, and goodness, ripening, evidently, as he lay there with a far-away look in his eyes, that saw then, only home and heaven.

And so it is with this whole harvest of life; it is infinitely vaster, as the harvest of the world is, than our estimate; and God is here to see to every grain of it, as Nature sees to every grain that lies in her lap from April to October.

> " God, the Creator, does not sit aloof,
> As in a picture painted on a roof,
> Occasionally looking down from thence, —
> He is all presence and all providence."

So it is again with the truth of variety. Men differ in their ways and in their nature as widely as the chestnut and cherry, or the walnut and the peach, and yet they may all be good men.

Here, again, we set up our idea of what is good fruit in the face of heaven, and then find it hard to make out that there is much good in the world. We want men and women to be good according to the way we define goodness, and cannot believe in them if they cannot conform to our standard. A man may be as good at the heart of him as a man can be; but if he be sharp or hard on the surface, we cannot quite believe in such goodness as that; we never think that such a man is a chestnut or a walnut in the harvest of the year, as good in his own way as any. Others, again, are all sweetness until you get at their heart, and then you find a tang of bitterness and hardness you never expected. You wonder whether they can be really good men. You might as well wonder whether there can be a good plum, or peach, or cherry. Some, again, are wrapped up in husks, that are dry, withered, and dead; but down within the husk is the grain, and that is good, and you know it; but you sorrow that the husk should be there, and never think it has to be there for a nature like that, or there would be no grain, and that by and by all this will be stripped away and done with.

The variety in the fruit of life is as divine as the abundance. Peter had a forbidding outside, with a heart as tender as ever beat; and John's heart, when you come close to him, was anything but tender; but they were both saints for all that. Erasmus was, perhaps, the most fascinating man of his day; Luther, to look at, one of the least. The good of Erasmus was more on the outside, of Luther, more within. They are both to be counted among the noblest children of God. Goldsmith was a pulp of a rare sweetness almost down at the core; Johnson had a goodness unspeakably different, but quite as good, in one of the knottiest and hardest shells to look at that was ever seen. Stephen Girard was a by-word for what was hard and keen; but once when the yellow fever raged in Philadelphia he was the first man in the town in his fearless devotion and sweet self-sacrifice for the sick and dying. We have one idea of goodness, Heaven has another.

In all sorts of husks and shells, hard, sharp, withered, and dead, God sees a goodness we are always missing, and counts and treasures it in the granary of heaven. We think of him too much as one walking through the world, looking only for the best, and rejecting, with aversion, what is not the best. I tell you when he goes forth with his reapers to gather his harvest, he looks as lovingly now as once he looked through the eyes of Christ, his Son, for all the good there is everywhere. There may be only a single grain in October where he put in a grain in March: he bids his angels gather that as carefully as if it were a hundred fold.

Then of the long ripening. The harvest we would have, if we had our way, would all be gathered in October. Our idea of Humanity is, that it should come to its end like corn fully ripe, or the apples that are only perfected in the frost, and we almost lay it up as a grudge against Heaven that we cannot have it so. But ever since the world was, Humanity has had its long ripening. Delicate blossoms have bloomed in the spring that could never live to summer. Little children, the snowdrops of the year, young men and maidens, the early summer fruit, strong men in their prime, perfected in August, — so the harvest of Humanity has grown and been gathered from first to last. It is hard to see, through our tears, that this can be the divine way with us, and the most blessed way Heaven could contrive for our blessing. But with little children in heaven, that passed away like the snowdrops, and youth that ripened in its June, and true friends and kinsfolk that were perfected in their August, and left me to wait for the early or the latter autumn, or the winter, I cling to the conviction that the long ripening was the divinest. I would have kept them all; my heart aches for them with an intolerable longing; sometimes I wonder how it can be that God will be justified when he speaks to me of his perfect providence and infinite love in taking these from me. He will not argue. He will only ask what I think my life would have been had they never come to bless me in their seasons, and then to be taken away. It will be all right when it comes to that.

This finally rounds itself with a word of admonition. First, that I shall not be content with my own poor limited vision of the harvest of Humanity. When I make my sense of the fullness, and variety, and ripening of men the standard with which to measure the divine sense of it, it is as if I made my sense of what is gathered here in October tell the whole story of the year all over the world. Good fruit to God surpasses all conception that I can form either of its measure or of its variety. Second, this must not for one instant leave me careless about growing to be my best, or of helping others to grow. It must only be an inspiration and incitement to me, as I feel there is so much more to encourage me than there would be if I believed that the most of what can be grown is only good to burn. It is good to garner under all its varieties. I shall not despair of anything. If only a little seed of good ripens, that little seed will never be lost. One of the worst women we ever had, says the matron of one of the great English prisons, was caught one day weeping over a daisy. Well, I think God's angels saw that woman weeping, and went and told it in heaven, and then there was joy there, for they knew that somehow, somewhere, some time, that "wee crimson tipped flower" would bring her, and be brought by her, through the golden gates.

It is not for a moment my idea, last of all, that because the great Husbandman will certainly make the best of the multitudes that are like the wild fruit of the wilderness, and of those that are like the smaller and more ordinary growth of the field and forest, and of all the rest we have been in the habit of leaving out of the measure of good fruit to God, — we are to be satisfied with anything short of the uttermost goodness, largeness, and ripeness we can possibly attain to. The worst farmer I ever knew, was a man who was always sure that his landlord would not trouble him about either rent or crop, because his family had been, time out of mind, in the sunshine of their lord's favor. It is always the danger of our confidence in God's providence, that we shall come to think it will be satisfied with our improvidence. Only as we make the best of what we have, and so become the best we can be, shall we win the great "well-done;" and no man or woman ought ever to be satisfied with anything less than to try for it. Patience, perseverance, good endeavor through storm and shine, the uplifted heart, the pure life, the large sympathy, the faith that was in Christ, and the truth, and the love, — these will bring into my own life an ever-ripening perfection, and save me from the poor perversity of thinking that God has not an infinite store of fruit as good as mine or better.

> " So will I gather strength and hope anew,
>   For I do know God's patient love perceives,
> Not what we did, but what we tried to do;
> And though the ripened ears be sadly few,
>   He will accept our sheaves."

V.

HOW ENOCH WALKED WITH GOD.

GEN. v. 22: "Enoch walked with God."

THE first part of my text is the most striking characterization of a good man's life to be found in our Bible; the last, the most touching record of a good man's end. It is said of other men, that they followed after God, or walked in the way of God; that this one died full of years, and that one satisfied; but it is reserved for this man alone to win and hold this great place — to walk with God as with a dear friend, voice answering to voice, hand touching hand, face reflecting face, from the beginning to the end of life; then, when the end comes, Death is shorn of his terrors, casting no more shadow on Enoch's spirit than if it were the spirit of a yearling child; the life that now is opening into that which is to come, as a clear twilight opens into day.

And it is not needful to tell you how blessed

such a life and death must be. I know you will agree with me, that no life can be more beautiful, no end more desirable. The most primitive characterization of a good man's life, this is still as much as can be said of any man, more than any man I have ever known would like to say of his own life, or predict of his death. And this is notable, because in this light the text is as good for what it teaches in doctrine, as for what it testifies to life. Because, if I inquire to-day after the essential conditions of a perfect walk with God, — what I must do to attain eternal life, — I am directed, in our common Christian teaching, to do at least five things: first, to study carefully my Bible; second, to come to God through his Son, Christ Jesus; third, to join the Christian church; fourth, to keep the Sabbath; and fifth, to observe the ordinances, such as the Lord's Supper. These are counted essential conditions to a perfect walk with God in our time. If I am faithful to four of them, I am not considered quite so good as if I keep the five. If I say church and sacrament are not essential, I am considered still more out of the true path. But if I then go on to say the Sabbath is not essential, — that a man may be saved in other ways than by faith in the personal and risen Christ, and that the Bible must be servant to the soul, not the soul to the Bible, — then Christian men tell me I cannot walk with God at all, and that my end will be a leap in the dark after a life in the dark, with dark faces all about me.

But I brush the dust away from this most honorable name, and ask what Enoch had of all this that is made so essential to me; and I find that he had no Bible, no knowledge of this personal Christ, no church, no Sabbath, and no sacraments; which brings me, by a very short and simple way, to this great truth; that all these things, — very good, never to be undervalued by any soundhearted man, — are not, after all, essential to the perfect life, or else Enoch had not been able to attain to this perfection before they were heard of; and that under these outward and visible signs there must be, therefore, some inward and spiritual grace, possessing which at any time, in any land, a man possesses all things — can walk with God as Enoch did, and find at the last that mortality is swallowed up in life.

What crumb of proof is needed to show that

Enoch was so destitute, can, of course, only be mentioned in the briefest way. That he had no Bible is clear, from the fact that if Moses wrote the first five books of it, Enoch himself had then been translated some two thousand years.

"After the most careful study of this question, we cannot infer that more than the simple weekly division of time was known before Moses," says the writer of the article "Sabbath," in Smith's great "New Bible Dictionary."

The claim that the obscure oracle,—that the seed of the woman should bruise the serpent's head,—must have been a revelation of the Redeemer, it is entirely impossible to believe. That Enoch could have belonged to a church, except as the church belonged to Enoch, when,

> "Kneeling down to heaven's eternal King,
> The saint, the father, and the husband prays,"

it is equally impossible to infer; while the time was yet very far distant when men should build up a stupendous ecclesiastical pretension, from the longing of the most loving heart that ever beat on this earth, to be remembered by friend and follower, even in the simple every-day usage of eating bread and drinking wine, to be blended as intimately with the spirit as these elements were with the materialism of their life. And I feel ready to apologize for offering even this brief hint of the proof, that not one of those things now considered so essential had then been heard of, until I remember how hard it was for me to realize once what is now so simple and self-evident; and how easy it is to slide into a semi-sense, that what is now made of such ponderous importance, was always so; and that we are doing some new thing when we establish a church like this, in which we declare much that others deem essential and supreme, to be but symbolic and subordinate, while, indeed, we are but backing up to the most absolute conservatism; bringing old things into the new time, as if we should sow, and reap from the Illinois prairie, wheat grains buried for uncounted centuries in some rock-tomb by the field.

I propose to discuss briefly this destitution of Enoch then; this poverty, by which he came so directly into the possession of the kingdom of heaven; to touch here and there these essentials of our times, and see how the man might have been richer or poorer for their presence in his life, and so, by consequence, see what they can be, and what they cannot be, to us.

First of all, Enoch had no Bible; and yet, sad as it seems to be without a Bible, it would depend very greatly on the man whether this destitution would be a blight or a blessing. I love the Bible supremely. In all the world I have found no book to set beside it. Other books I love well. Milton, Taylor, Carlyle, Tennyson, Emerson, Spencer, and many a noble name beside in this great brotherhood are so dear to me, that there are few sacrifices I could not gladly make rather than lose their companionship. But when I am in any great strait — when I want to find words other than my own to rebuke some crying sin or to stay some desperate sinner, to whisper to the soul at the parting of the worlds, or to read, as I sit with them that weep beside their dust, words that I know will go to the right place as surely as corn dropped into good soil on a gleaming May day, — then I put aside all books but one — the book out of which my mother read to me, and over which she sang to me, as far back as I can remember; and when I take this book, it is like those springs that never give out in the dryest weather, and never freeze in the hardest, because they reach so directly into the great, warm fountains hidden under the surface. It never fails.

But have we not all noticed the curious fact, that men go to the Bible for what they want to find, rather than what they ought to find? that those who profess the most absolute submission to its authority, offer generally the finest possible illustration of the supremacy of the soul over the Bible, in the way they contrive to make it serve their turn? and that it is by no means impossible to find duplicates of the good Scotchwoman's minister, of whom she said, "If there is a cross text in the Bible, he is sure to find it, and take it for a sermon."

The truth is, the Bible is like a great pasture, into which you turn all manner of feeders. The horse takes what he wants, so does the cow; the sheep is true to its instinct, so is the goat; and then, last of all, the ass rolls the thistle, like a sweet morsel, under his tongue. So, when a man with a large, sweet nature, comes to the Bible, he crops, by a sure instinct, all the large, sweet passages. The hopeful man finds the hopeful things; the sad man the sorrowful things; the hard man, the hard things; and every man the things that satisfy his craving, though they may in no way make for his peace. If, then, Enoch was a right-hearted man, the Bible would have been a wonderful blessing to his life. It would have whispered consolation in his trouble; it would have rebuked him with a sad sternness for his sin; it would have refreshed him many a time in his weariness; it would have helped him to be a man. But if he had been hard, narrow, bitter, and bigoted, it might have confirmed him in all that is most ugly and unlovable in a man otherwise intending to do right, and been compelled by him, as it has been by so many, into antagonism to the purest and best things. Make the Bible minister to such a spirit as this; find in it merely hard, bitter things, to confirm a hard bitter tone towards all but those that happen to belong to your own particular Bethel; find nothing to make you tender and kind to the good men who may happen to be more radical or conservative than yourselves in their interpretation of the essentials of the truth and life, then you are infinitely poorer with a Bible than Enoch was without one.

Because we cannot afford to forget, that this man, walking with God, was by no means so destitute as he seems; but being a man whose soul was open to the heavens, out of which whatever is best in our Bible has come, he had in some way a Bible after all,—an Old and New Testament that was never permitted to grow dusty, that was not brought merely for good manners where the minister happened to be staying over night, but a Bible fresh and perennial, beyond what most of us that set such store by our Bible can imagine. It is surely no light matter in the discussion of this question, to remember that this perfect life was all done when the world was young; that this man lived while men yet believed angels descended with sweet silence on the mountains; when the things which were afterwards put into the book of Job and the older Psalms were glistening in the dew of the sun newly risen on the race; when the pure wonder and trust of childhood had not gone out of men; when, believing that the morning stars sang together, all the sons of God shouted for joy.

What Enoch had then, came to him directly. If, in any rude runic or hieroglyphic way, he had possession of the story of the struggles of his race to work out their own salvation, he read his Cotton Mather and Winthrop, his Bancroft and Hildreth, and Frank Moore, in a near, sacred, very present sense of the presence of God in the struggle, that we do not now understand, and that we never can understand, until we dare believe that, when we want to read in our church or family some great lesson from history, these annals of our own are so significant that we can take a chapter from any one of them, and read it with a reverence as deep and all-pervading as that we feel when we read in the books of Moses, or in the chronicles of the judges and kings.

When Enoch lived, if his melons were large, and sweet, and plentiful, he thanked God for good melons. We say, I was very particular about seed and soil. If his trees flourished exceedingly, they hinted some blessed thing about God's good providence to a tree. I remember that I sent for the plants all the way to Rochester. When Enoch lived, and flowers carpeted dale and upland on the Euphrates, he thought as the poet sang, how

> "Not worlds on worlds in phalanx deep,
>   Need we to prove that God is here;
> The daisy, fresh from Nature's sleep,
>   Tells of his hand in lines as clear.
> For who but he who arched the skies,
>   And poured the day-spring's living flood,
> Wonders alike in all he tries,
>   Could raise the daisy's purple bud,
> Mould its green cup, its wiry stem,
>   Its fringéd border nicely spin,
> And cut the gold embosséd gem,
>   That, set in silver, gleams within,
> And fling it unrestrained and free
>   O'er hill, and dale, and desert sod,
> That man, where'er he walks, may see
>   In all his footsteps there's a God."

Our children come to us with flowers, but they treat us to scientific dissections of them, and laugh at the dear old names we give them. We are very proud, of course, as becomes the fathers of little persons so learned, and say to ourselves, "This is very wonderful!" But then, we cannot but wonder whether they do see quite so much in the wild rose or the bluebell as I did when I strayed to seek them by bank and hedge-row, before I had heard of such things as Latin and botany, or dreamed that somewhere in the preexisted heavens were voices training to call me father. Enoch lived when what sense of sin and retribution lay in the soul touched it to the very quick; when dyspepsia and gout were not to be explained away by a pleasant doctor, but meant over-feeding and under-work; when the words we sing out of David's psalms, how "the heavens declare the glory of God, and the firmament showeth his handiwork," were singing themselves in Enoch's heart; when heaven and earth, and life, and the life to come, lay near and next to the soul of the man that walked with God; when every babe born into his house was a chapter in a New Testament, teaching some new wonder of the truth and life; and what it is to be a child of God, was made all clear to him in his own children.

Now, this Bible was open to Enoch, as it is open to every man who will look into it. And when we think of this, we cannot wonder that he should do so well before teachers of the truth had begun to confound the light which lighteth every man that cometh into the world, with one of its most blessed results; to make this mighty aid to the perfect life and up-springing end, one of its most essential conditions; " to soil the book in struggles for the binding;" to practically deny that in all ages, they that fear God and work righteousness are accepted of him, or that the invisible things of him from the creation of the world are clearly seen, being set forth by the things that are made. A voice that always commands attention, has hinted that the highest faith of this soul is to centre finally in the Bible or in Mathematics. It is possible; and yet we may remember to-night the high faith of this soul, while Bible and probably Mathematics too were yet invisible, and then be as sure as we are sure God is very God and our Father, that if ever Mathematics shall come to assume so great a place as to divide the kingdom with this great book, and win souls to trust in them as the very truth, then will they somehow become the very life too, and the properties and proportions of number be so filled with a divine beauty, so clothed in robes of light, that men will grow brave and strong, and weep and rejoice as they study them; will be martyrs and confessors for their truth and life, as surely as ever men were martyrs and confessors for the truth and life in the Prophecies and Gospels.

The time which I have given to a special consideration of this one thing, will release me from the discussion of those other so-called essentials with any like elaboration. I cannot well tell you what a blessed light has come into my life from the face of Jesus Christ since the old times, when, one by one, the dark shadows that had always fallen between his life and mine began to lift. And I will give place to no man again in true love to a true church; to some common home where men and women meet who are drawn together by a mutual love; where they can no more help meeting than our children can help rushing home from school; a sort of divine brotherhood, in which every man feels some sorrow when trouble falls to any, and a common interest in each great joy; a church so true, that if you dishonor one, you dishonor every one, and that any man may be sure his good name is safe while one is within ear-shot who worships in that place; a church where great reservoirs of power are filled full and held ready to be poured out whenever the true occasion comes to open the flood-gates for God or man, and yet where there is such a continual overflow, that the store is kept sweet by its own generous flowing; a church where whatsoever things are true are welcome, and where there is such a constant deepening of the spiritual life manifested in the devout utterances of all in prayers and praises, that every man is lifted nearer heaven at his need than he could hope to be by solitary meditation.

And the Sabbath I love. It may be a superstition; but the more I study the question of seven-sameness, the more I am drawn to the Sabbath as a prime necessity of life, apart from its special uses for worship, and ready to admit that, if it did not take so great a place in the master book of the master races on the globe, we should still grope our way somehow to the conclusion of a great physiologist, that "while the night's rest seems to equalize the circulation, still it does not restore the perfect balance to the life." Hence it will come to pass, that while the man who neglects to take a seventh day, at least, for rest, may be borne along by the vigor of his mind to continual exertion, yet in the long run he will break down sooner and more suddenly than the man who is determined to put aside at least one seventh of his working life for rest and recreation. But not for this alone will the Christian minister stand by the Sabbath, but because he knows that the needs of the soul are as imperative as those of the body, the hunger of the inner life as sore as that of the outer, and that no man can live by bread alone.

There is no sight in this world so touching to me, as the sight of this church on a Sunday. I look down the aisles, and there see the lawyer, who has been wrangling in the courts; the merchant, who has been watching the fluctuations of the market; the mechanic, every day driven by clanging hammer and grinding wheel; the maiden, weary with the incessant task-work of the school; and the mother, nearly worn out by the heavy cares of the home. But here they all gather; and as their faces turn to me, I see no longer the busy man and woman, but the soul returning to its rest; coming to God, if haply it may feel after him, and find him; endeavoring to shift the burden, so that the pinch will not be quite so much on the one place; striving to find how they that wait upon the Lord shall renew their strength; and, last of all, while I believe that the sacrament of the Lord's Supper has managed to drift to the farthest possible point from its primitive intention; to become so thin and shadowy in its material elements, that I almost wish these could be dispensed with, as they are so nearly; there is that at the heart of it, when I meet with the few who feel that it is to them a great consolation, that makes me almost forget I am eating a crumb of bread and sipping a drop of wine, I can enter so nearly with them into that dear Presence, and so realize how wonderful was this sacrifice, made in his perfect prime, by one who shrank from death in that way, as possibly humanity never shrank before, yet would make no hair's breadth of compromise to save his life, though when the horror of great darkness fell, he felt that even God had forsaken him.

But I should fall back on Enoch, and insist on using his Bible, and no other, if I were compelled to choose between that and the thorns and thistles so many well-meaning men insist on my accepting, whether I will or not, and assimilating into my nature as the bread of life; as I would shut the book, and never open it again, rather than be compelled to acquiesce in the one hideous monstrosity of an eternal hell fire — so, if it were possible for me to be beaten out of my belief in this dear Christ, as he now looks at me out of heaven; to see in him mainly a sacrifice to slake the wrath of an angry God; or a being holding a relation to God that contradicts every possibility of nature or numbers; or even were I required to bind myself over to believe what contradicted the best insight of my own soul concerning his life, death, and resurrection, whether this chorded most nearly with this or that side of liberal Christianity; or if I were compelled to join a church in which men and women who compose it are as much isolated from a common Christian fellowship as if the cord that should bind them was electricity, and they were sitting in pews of glass, where not my own honest, natural bent was respected, and not the discharge of daily duties, in a simple, loving spirit, was counted religion, but I was compelled to do things against my nature, not daring to refuse, in peril of my soul; or if I were compelled to keep a Sabbath again, so that I durst not say to any man who has been so chained to his desk all the week that he has never taken a full breath,

"My friend, I am set to watch for your soul; and as a minister of the Gospel of that Christ, who said the first consideration is not the Sabbath, but the man, I tell you that this is not the true worship for you to come here, cramping yourself every Sunday over your Bible and hymn-book; the true worship, the Sabbath-keeping most sacred, will be to intersperse with your Sundays at church, Sundays when you will start out on a long-stretching walk into the country, or go lie down, through a summer day, on your back at the root of a tree, and look up into the great, quiet heavens; when you will do something that will expand your natural life, and sweeten and reform it; that will take the snarl out of your brain, instead of letting me put another into it through my sermon:" if I were compelled again to accept the sacrament as a sort of occult charm, instead of a sacred remembrance; to invest it with frightful possibilities of damnation if I do not succeed, before I take it, of divesting myself of everything that is most bright, cheerful, and human—then, rather than be bound so to Bible, Intercessor, Church, Sabbath, or Sacrament, I would go back and range with good old Enoch, free, self-contained, subject to God alone, as He speaks to me through nature and the soul. Then, if any man troubled me with impertinences about the soundness of my faith, and its power to bear me through life and death — if no deeper argument were worth my while, I would refer him to this primitive instance out of his own prime authority, how one, doing by one necessity what I am doing by another, won this supreme glory and blessing, — that he walked with God, and was translated, so that he should not see death.

All this I say, finally, not because I would take one atom of power, and riches, and wisdom, and strength, and honor, and glory, and blessing from these aids to religion, but because I would make them everything they can be, as ministering angels to the soul, and yet be sure that the power by which a man shall walk with God preceded them, informs them, surpasses them, and is so full and free that it overflows all churches, books and created beings, as if you should set as many vessels in a fountain of living water. It is like the sun that fills a cup of every flower in your gardens, and yet fills just as full every wild flower on the boundless prairies: blesses me when I bend, worshipping in spirit and in truth, on Gerizim or Zion; when I gather my children around me as Enoch did, to tell them that the great God who made this green valley, this shining river and sandy desert, who holds those far blue mountains fast on their sunless pillars, and folds the sparrow to its rest out on the slender branch under the stars, — this God is their Father and mine: touches me when I meet some kindred soul, or walk alone in the shadow of great woods, and commune of those ever-fresh mysteries of life and the life to come, while the birds sing in the branches, and the sun shoots down shafts of splendor, or the clouds gather, and the thunders shake the great boles, awing me into a silence more sacred than our most sacred speech; or, when I find a man who can say words that make me step out more stoutly and steadily, who will turn a grave, sweet face of pity to me when I stumble, will lift me out of the dust when I fall, will lend me a shoulder when I am weary, will make me feel that there is at least one true soul abroad in the world, walking with God, listening to His voice, touching His hand,

and sure whenever the time shall come for him to be taken up, to reveal some new hint of heaven, as he turns his face for a moment ere he enters within the portal.

Now, this is what we are trying to establish and maintain, this most primitive and yet most perennial faith; to see in these most blessed things, not the masters, but the servants of the soul; to hold all questions of Bible, Intercessor, Church, Sabbath, and Sacrament as the means of grace, but not the end. God is the end of all our worship and service; and we want to build this faith into a power massive enough to stand impregnable against all the assaults of the devil, under every guise; and may the God that walked with Enoch walk with us and help us in this purpose.

We want free churches in this free land — churches that are strong, yet delicate; massive, but tender; Christ-like and constant, gracious and good. And we want all who are one with us in this purpose to join hands and help us. Every large, free thinker should stand by such freedom; every believer in God, not as shut up in a corner and hemmed in by these fire-bars, but as in the whole world, with all men for his children, should be glad of such a faith; and I doubt not but the time is coming when this will be the universal religion. We must work for that time, give our money for it, our labor, and, if need be, our life.

VI.

THE HOLINESS OF HELPFULNESS.

Rom. xii. 11: "Not slothful in business, fervent in spirit, serving the Lord."

GEORGE STEPHENSON was getting ready to go to Methodist meeting. He was a young man, just at that period in life when young men go to Methodist meeting more and more until they are brought directly under the influence of the master-spirit of the place, and become in a sense religious men. There is not much doubt in my mind, as I read this young man's life up to this time, that he is in a fair way to that preferment. He has that thread of natural piety and goodness in his nature that is almost sure to draw him into a more intimate relation with the forms and industries of the recognized religious life about him, if nothing prevent. I said he was getting ready to go to the meeting, when a neighbor came to tell him he was wanted. He was then running an engine at a coal-pit. There was another pit between this and his home, which he passed every day, that had been flooded with water, so that the men were beaten out. The company got a steam-pump to clear the pit, and kept it at work for twelve months, with no success at all. The water, when they had been pumping twelve months, was as deep as when they first began to pump, and the wives and children were starving for bread.

This young Stephenson had a most active energy and fervent spirit towards whatever went by steam. The great ambition of his boyhood was to run an engine; and when he rose to that position, as he did very soon — for it is a cheering fact, that while a man may long for a hundred things and not get one, a boy hardly ever fails to accomplish *his* purpose if he has a genuine hunger to be, or to do, some particular thing, — when this boy rose to the position he wanted, he treated his engine as if he loved her. Whenever there was a holiday and the works were stopped, instead of going out with the rest, he studied her until she became as familiar to him as his own right hand. He was not slothful in business, and he was fervent in spirit. Intimate with the charge that was laid upon him, he soon began to perceive why those women and children were starving. The difference between what the pump was, and what it ought to be, was the difference between a tall, slender, narrow-chested man and a short, sturdy, broad-chested man, engaged in digging earth or scooping out water. Every pump owner in the country-side had tried to mend this pump and failed, — because, I suppose, pump-mending and engine-running with them was a business and not a passion. This young man, with the fervent spirit, said one day, as he went past the pit, "I can clear that pit in a week;" and they laughed him to scorn. But they could not laugh the water to scorn; and so at last they sent for him to come and try his hand. He went there instead of going to the church. He went into the pit on a Sunday morning, and worked all that day, and until the next Sunday, cleared out all the water in a week, and sent the men down to earn their children bread.

From that time the young man comes into notice. He works through all sorts of opposition, and never rests until he has got an engine to run fifty miles an hour. He is, more than any other man, entitled to be called the Father of the railroad system. He kept the diligent hand and fervent heart right on to the end of his life. He was a good husband, a good father, a good friend, and a good citizen. But it is a curious fact that, from the time when he was prevented from going to meeting on that Saturday night, he never seems to have gone, or to have thought of going again, to the end of his life. He did not turn religious, as we say, even when he had nothing else to do, but lived a kindly, sunny, or shadowy, faithful life, right on to the end, and then died quietly, and made no sign. He never said he feared he had done wrong in turning from that church to that coal-pit, and trying to mend the pump Sunday, instead of keeping the Sabbath day holy by doing nothing; indeed, it never seems to have occurred to him to think the matter over in any way whatever: his heart was too full, and his hand too busy about engines, to find room for the idea; to find time, as we should say, to save his soul. And so it brings up a question, that to me has a good deal of interest, namely: While this man was so busy and so fervent in the way I have noted, did he also serve the Lord? or, from the moment he turned aside from the meeting, and began to lose that sense and liking for meetings, and their peculiar services, did he cease to serve the Lord altogether, and remaining only diligent in business and fervent in spirit, go out of this world into darkness and despair?

Now, I am well aware what the common answer to such a question would be: it would be, " We must leave him in the hands of God ; we cannot answer the question, because we have no data." But that is not true. If he had been an idle good-for-nothing, a scampish sharper, an abandoned libertine, an unprincipled truckler, or a political vulture ; if he had beaten his wife, trained up his child in the way he should go — to state's prison; if he had been a common nuisance for sixty-nine years and a half, never going into a church except to make a disturbance, never keeping the Sabbath except in sensual sleep, and six months before his death, or six weeks, or six days, had repented of his sin, had led a good and pure life, adopted religious ideas like those commonly held, and said clearly that he believed God had pardoned his sins, and would take him to heaven, we should feel the utmost confidence of that man's safety from that date. But we do not feel sure for this other man. It is a great mystery, and we must leave him in the hands of God. But if you push us to the fair conclusion of our own standard of religious belief, and the books we adopt, we feel compelled to say that he has gone to hell.

Now this looks to me like a tremendous piece of injustice on the very face of it. I think if a man could be brought face to face with the question as I have stated it, and as it really stands in the common theological systems; could see these men brought up before what are called our Evangelical churches, having never heard of these peculiar religious ideas up to that time; could see the men examined, and then observe which man was sent upward and which downward by these standards, his conclusion would be, that there was something radically wrong in their premises; and I can well imagine how such a man would argue for a new trial. He would say, "I know nothing at all about your authorities for this curious decision. You tell me that they bear the mint mark of divinity; that they have come to you from the remotest antiquity; from kings, and prophets, and apostles, and the Son of God himself; that they are the fruit of a divine inspiration, foreshadowed in prophecies, confirmed by miracles, and held by martyrs at the stake." Now all this may be true; but I know something of the laws of this Universe, — of what enters into the real life of man for blessing and for hurt. I cannot, and I will not, deny the claim of this man, who has kept the divine law six months out of threescore and ten years, to be saved. It is always right to do right; and a man is bound upward from the moment when he does begin to do well. Whenever that may be, he begins to come out of his rags and wretchedness into a wholesome purity and happiness. But where you have one reason on your authorities for saying that this man is good and ascended, because he has done what you say for six months out of the threescore and ten years of his life, I have six score and twenty good reasons for the assurance that this other man is also ascended, because he has done good according to the organic laws of the world ever since he came into it.

Now, be sure I have not brought up this question only to prove that the man I have mentioned for illustration was saved,— though the common interpreters of the Christian doctrine claim that by their standards it is impossible he should be saved,— but to make the man, as he represents an idea of very great importance in our life, the basis of some discussion of a segment, at least, of true religion.

And I say a segment, because religion in all its reaches is as boundless as the Spirit of God, and the infinitely varied life of man can make it, and there can be no exhaustive system of religion, in the hard, dry sense of the term. Every system is a statement, a proposition, a shadow of the principles that impress most deeply the man who makes it. The Calvinist has not the same idea of Free Grace the Arminian has, nor the Arminian the same idea of Predestination the Calvinist has. The Episcopalian, and Quaker, and Presbyterian have no common union except that which comes from standing at the angles of a triangle as far as possible apart. The men who sprinkle, and the men who immerse, and the men who do neither, can all show exhaustive reason for their particular methods. And I think the reason for all this lies far less in the perverseness of the men, than in their powerlessness to see all the glory and grandeur of the truth of God that is in the world.

Schools of theology are like schools of painting — they are in some measure the copy of a copy. They copy from their great master, and he copied from God. Walking down the world of truth and beauty, the great painter sees things that make his soul aflame with their beauty and wonder: mountains, meadows, woodlands, rivers, men and women, sun and shadow, fill him with a sense of their intimate, unutterable divinity. But he cannot paint all he sees; he can paint really very little, but he paints what he can — he follows the bent of his own genius and inspiration; he brings in here a meadow, and there a wood; here a mountain, and there a river; here a flower, and there a figure; here a bit of marvellous sunlight, and there a wonderful touch of shadow; and makes them all glorious or sombre in the coloring of his own soul, and when the picture is done, those that love it and follow it, declare that it exhausts all perfection. But beautiful as it may be, the man has got in but a very small piece of the infinite beauty that is all about him. And so it is in religious truth: no one system exhausts even the Bible; how much less the boundless wealth of truth, of which the Bible is but the part of a record. The system may be a good thing for the men who love that method, trying faithfully to copy the great original who founded the school; the copyist in the one case will hardly need write under his composition, "This is a mountain," and "This is a man," any more than in the other he will need to say, "I am religious, after the school of Calvin or Luther." Still the Rembrandt splendors of Calvin, the sober-gray realism of Fox, the water-color landscape of our Baptist brother, the broad Hogarths of Wesley, true to exaggeration, the sunny Claude-like pictures of Channing, the often stern Salvator pieces of Parker, and the rich composition of the Episcopal, which in some lights seem to rise to the beauty and truth of the best Turners, and in other lights to descend to the stage effects of Martin, and of which no one seems to be sure about the original, or whether there be one — all these are true in their way to what the master saw — a transcript of things that filled his soul with keen delight, or holy rapture, or awful solemnity. But beyond them, and above them, and all about them, were other meadows "beautiful as the gardens of the angels upon the slopes of Eden, other forests that cover the mountains like the shadow of God, other rivers that move like his own eternity."

. And so the claim that not one of the sects, nor all the sects together, have exhausted the truth, brings the claim of this man into court to come in for a share, not of salvation only in the life to come, but of glory in the best, the most religious sense, in the life that now is, though he did take such a singular stand. When my friends said to me while yet a Methodist preacher, "How can you preach for Dr. Furness, in Philadelphia, who is a Unitarian? we should suppose you could not find anything to say that these people would listen to, and yet be true to your Methodism;" I replied, "I find it easier to preach to them than to preach at home; for I leap over the fence that bounds the system of Methodism, and as they are already over the fence that has bounded the system of Unitarianism, we all meet in the boundless world of truth and beauty which God has made outside, and it is wonderful how much we find to talk about when we get there."

I think the vital point in the question at issue turns on whether, what a man thinks and feels, or what he does, is to be considered the essential element in his life. Whether certain ideas, feelings, and industries in relation to what we agree to call religion, are to be counted the great elements in the nobility of this life, and the safety of the life to come; or whether to do faithfully, with or without them, the one good thing which the passionate heart of the man indicates that he was created to do, is the true way to live.

I think also the honest verdict of the human heart turns to the deed; and I picked up a remarkable illustration of this, when once I was called to a place named Constantine, in Michigan, to attend the funeral of a gentleman I had known. He was a good man, but he made no profession of religion; never went to church; kept aloof from all sects. He had been for some time in delicate health, so that it was dangerous for him to travel in bad weather; when just in the twilight of one of the most terrible spring nights, he was summoned to Lansing, to consult on the impending rebellion. His wife tried to keep him home until morning; but he felt he must go. He went, and never held his head up after. In my sermon I pointed out the organic elements in the life of a man; how holily he may live as a father and husband and friend; mentioned how my hearers knew the record our friend had made, and touched on the grandeur of the last deed in which he gave his life, and then said, "Is not this religion?" I was the first man holding this faith openly, who had ever spoken there, but it was touching to see how readily those men and women caught the idea, with what joy they received it, and how they thanked me for confirming what had been in their hearts as a natural and necessary idea.

And once after this I visited Camp Douglas, and sat down on the cot of a sick man, a prisoner from the South. He said, "Are you a minister?" I answered, "Yes." "What sort, Baptist?" "No." "Methodist?" "No." "Presbyterian?" I wanted to see how far he knew, and so still said, "No." I suppose these were all he had ever heard about, for he opened his eyes wide, when he had exhausted his catalogue, and said, "What then?" I answered, "Unitarian." "Ah," said he, "I never heard of that before. What do they believe?" So I told him how they believe God is our Father, and cares for us every one, and how he takes a man for what he is rather than for what he says, and how after death he is just as much our Father as he was before. "Well," said the man, "I never heard that before; but that's right; come see me again." I went, I think, on the third day, but his cot was empty; he had gone to the Father.

John Ruskin, in one of his chapters on Modern Painters, enters into a discussion of the meanings of help. He says the clouds may come together, but they are no help to each other, and so the removal of one part is no injury to the rest, but if you take the sap or bark or pith from a plant, you do that plant essential injury, for the part you take away has taken hold on that power we call life, by which all things in the plant help each other; take a part from that power so that it cannot help the rest, and it becomes what we call dead. Then he says, if you take a limb from an animal, it is a far greater injury than to take a limb from a tree, because intensity of life is intensity of helpfulness; the more perfect the help the more dreadful the loss; the more intense the life the more terrible the corruption, and most terrible of all in a man, because his life is the most helpful and most intense of all. And so he ranges through this great thought until he finds that the name, which of all others is most expressive of the being of God, is that of the Helpful One, or, in our softer Saxon, the Holy One.

Now to me, this expresses exactly the idea that underlies life. The helpful life is the holy life. Holiness is help; sin is hinderance. At whatever point we touch life to help it, in whatever way we help the world and do not hinder it, whether by our prayers, and songs, and sermons, and industry in the church, or by the creation of a locomotive, or the construction of a railroad, or the painting of a picture, or the writing of a book, or the digging of a drain, or the forging of a horse-shoe, or the fighting of a battle — in whatsoever thing we do, if we really help and do not hinder, then that is a holy life. And in whatever way we hinder the world, and stand in the way of its life, its healthy, hearty growth, by doing what will hurt or hinder men in the largest sense, then that, being the reverse of helpful, is a sinful life. The first principles of sin and holiness reach back into all creeds and churches so far as they stand true to life, and no more; and the ultimate touchstone of holiness is the organic law by which the best interests of the whole man can be secured in his relation to the whole world, and all the men that are in it.

And there is a beautiful illustration of this principle in two related incidents in the life of Christ. When he sat down weary at the well, the Samaritan woman came to fill her pitcher, and entering into conversation with him, found that she had got hold of a preacher or prophet, and thinking to get a solution of the old vexed question, as to which was the true religion, Samaritan or Jew, said, " Our fathers worshipped in this mountain, and ye say that in Jerusalem men ought to worship." He replied, " Ye worship ye know not what; we know what we worship, for salvation is of the Jews." But when he heard the story, or saw in some inward way, how a man went down from Jerusalem to Jericho and fell among thieves, who stripped him and wounded him and left him for dead, and how two Jews, a priest and a Levite, men who stood first among the Jews in the relation of true church worship, — if praying and singing be true worship, — when he saw them go over to the other side, and leave the helpless man to his fate, and saw one of those Samaritans come along, who did not know what they worshipped, saw him leap from his horse in a great flood of pity and mercy, hold up the poor fellow's head, stanch his wounds, set him on his own beast and trudge along on foot himself, as if there was not a robber within a thousand miles, carry him to a tavern, and not throw him on the county when he got there, but pledge himself to pay all the expenses, and then walk away as if he had done one of the most common things in the world, — the great soul saw past the old dogma, into this fresh organic law, this universal principle of worship, this holiness of helpfulness, and his soul clave to the soul of the Samaritan who knew not God.

And be sure this principle underlies every other principle whatever in the religious life. I can teach God really just so far as I am good. Christ will be divine greatly by my divinity. I am my own proof, before letters, of the intrinsic worth of human nature. I shall not have much trouble in proving to a man God is our Father, if I can prove to him I am his brother. That volume of the Evidences of Christianity which the other side never did answer, and never will, is a book written on what the apostle calls the fleshly tables of the heart.

And this is the grand use of churches, systems, sacraments, and ceremonies. They reach back into the principle of helpfulness to find their seal; they are centres of help to the world, and to the man, or they are nothing. I care not one pin for their age, evidences, liturgies, theologies. If the church that holds them and holds you, cannot help you, do not go to it. If it does help you, do not dare to stay away, when you need help; and that, I take it, with most of us, is pretty much all the time. If your church does not help others, let it perish. If it does, care for it as you care for every noble and helpful thing: nay, care for it as the noblest. If the liberal Christian preacher here, or anywhere, cannot help you in your most central and sacred life, and the Catholic bishop can, then I charge you, on your allegiance to God and your own soul, go to the bishop by the shortest route; but if we do help you, if our words and deeds touch some spring, that is to all the rest of your manhood what the mainspring is to a watch, if we help you to a clearer vision and a deeper trust, to a fairer hope and a more abundant helpfulness, then we take hold on first things; we stand to you in the old apostolic relation; we carry the keys, the bishop does not; and every such man is the rock on which the Master will build his church, and the gates of hell shall not prevail against it.

Here, then, was the great use of the man I have noted for illustration — his place in the world was not in the church, but in the foundery — he was not the heart, but the hand in the body of Christ; but he was the hand, and his mission was to be strong, diligent, faithful, true to his trust, and let all the rest take care of itself. God raised him up to inaugurate railroads; woe to him if he does not do that. He will endanger his soul if he neglects that. His place on that Sunday was in the coal-pit; woe to him if the Master comes and finds him in the Methodist meeting.

The great problem for him to solve is, not whether he is going to be happy in meeting, or happy on his death-bed, or happy at all on this earth, but if he is going to be helpful in the one supreme way in which God has made him to be helpful. If he cannot be a true husband, and father, and friend, and man, and machine-maker, except he belong to the church, then at his peril he fails to join one. If the church and its religious ideas, emotions, and inspiration are needed to make him a good man, if he is not brave, faithful, strong, and loving, and the church can aid him to be all that, as I believe it can, then he must seek the church; but if all that is in him, then God is in him to will and to do of His good pleasure, and when he carries that locomotive up to the throne, God will say, "Well done."

There can be no more striking and conclusive proof of where the claim ought to rest for the intrinsic worth of that, for the lack of which most religious teachers are conscientiously compelled to send such men as Stephenson to the pit, than to notice the way in which the war tried them, as by fire. It is a most striking study. From 1857 to 1861 the whole land went under a great tide of revival. From Chicago, our Young Men's Christian Association went to New Orleans, joined there in prayers and praises. It was but one instance in a thousand. The entire religious world was one. But when the South seceded, the church seceded with the state, and then came the wonder. These men held precisely the same religious beliefs and dogmas, uttered the same prayers and received the same sacraments as they had always done; and they found that those things would work as solidly to inspire treason as truth. "When Massa Jackson pray all night," his body servant said, "den I pack his tings; I know he go on a raid." Our great dead friend, our father Abraham, noticed this in our darkest days, and said, the rebels prayed a great deal, and to all appearances, with the best results. So can the wine the Samaritan takes to restore the dying man on the road to Jericho, madden the robber to murder them both. It is only in being true and right, in being on the side of truth, and justice, and humanity, only in reaching back into first things and being a helper there, that then God will be true, and every man godlike, whose life is of that noble grain.

And so ideas, emotions, creeds, meetings, sacraments, and ceremonies are all good as they do good : but they are as passive as the powder which, for ought I know, came out of the one cask to slay our father Abraham, and the wretched murderer by whose hand he fell. It is a weighty thing to me, that Christ makes those men, to whom he tells us he will say, " Come ye blessed," entirely unconscious that the things they had done were in any particular way religious. To be sure they had visited prisons, fed the hungry, clothed the naked, and tended the sick; but then what religion was there about that any more than in the Samaritan's saving the life of that dying Jew? That was merely humanity, helpfulness, morality. But the prayers the man said when he got back to Mount Gerizim, the purifications and praises he went through there, these were his religion. I have no doubt that they did help him, that they inspired him, and kept his heart fresh to do just so next time. But the thing he did, and not the belief he held, or the prayers he said, or the day he observed — the thing he did was his religion; the helpfulness of the man was his holiness, as it will be to those to whom Christ will say, "Well done;" while on the other side, those to whom he will say, "Depart ye cursed," are the men who will cry, "Did we not teach in thy name, and cast out devils, and work wonders?" But he will say, "Depart; I never knew you. You preached and did wonders, but you did not help." And so entirely does this helpfulness make our holiness, that the same deep and strong principle is made to reach across the worlds, and in the life to come, to give the faithful helper more power to help, as the best gift of God in heaven. The poet sings of a noble man dead, —

"How can we doubt that for one so true
There must be other nobler work to do?"

The Lord says, "Well done; thou hast been ruler over ten pounds, I will make thee ruler over ten cities."

And so I would affirm and rejoice in a church broad enough to take into full membership and full communion all those men who may never come inside the church doors, who never do a hand's turn at church work, who know nothing of our belief or practices, but whose whole heart, and soul, and mind, and strength, are devoted to some piece of helpfulness that shall lift this dark world into the sun; — wherever that man may be working the part of him that sent him, whether at the anvil, like my own father, or at the foot of Missionary Ridge, charging up hill like my adopted son, or resting for a moment to watch the mimic life on the stage with Abraham Lincoln; let the Angel of Death come ever so suddenly, cast over them his white robe and whisper peace, that place in which he finds them is the very nearest point to heaven; and the first word that greets them is the glad " Well done." And I would have all such true and faithful men know this; would fain say to them, " This that you are doing is work for God; you may be a saint of God in the place where you stand."

Friends, a mere feeling may fail you, but a helpful spirit never can, because that is a holy spirit. The ready hand and the fervent heart, if the one work and the other beat for good, is sure to be right. You mothers may be occupied with work for your children in the house, until you have no time for what you call religion; you men may not know which way to turn in consequence of business in the office, and you may wonder whether so much to do in this world is safe for the next; you may long for the forms and feelings that are counted of such importance in many churches. Now do not misunderstand me : if they would help you to be more helpful, you cannot get too many. But if they stand instead of your helpfulness, so that in feeling happy you think you are religious, and are not helpful, they are dangerous, and they may come to be deadly.

You may die, as this man did, at the close of a long, faithful, helpful life, and give no sign; and yet no understanding soul will doubt that, for one so true there must be other nobler work to do; or you may die, with a testimony shining like burnished gold, at the end of a life in which you did not even drive away the dogs from the beggar at your gate, but you will wake up in the torment of an unsatisfied soul, and go into the hell of lost opportunities.

And if you say, "I am hedged about, I can do nothing; I fain would help, but I cannot," — your very longing is help. "They also serve who only stand and wait." It is never true that we are not helpers; where the fervent heart is, there is the servant of God, and unto him comes ever with the work the reward. He is still and strong in God, because he is a co-worker with God, and his life holds for itself a secret which is not known to another — he has come in his very work to the rest that remaineth.

> "Abou Ben Adhem (may his tribe increase)
> Awoke one night from a deep dream of peace,
> And saw within the shadow of his room,
> Making it rich, like a lily in bloom,
> An angel writing in a book of gold.
> Exceeding peace had made Ben Adhem bold,
> And to the presence in the room he said,
> 'What writest thou?' The vision raised its head,
> And with a look made of all sweet accord,
> Answered, 'The names of those who love the Lord!'
> 'And is mine one?' asked Abou. 'Nay, not so,'
> Replied the angel. Abou spoke more low,
> But cheerly still, and said, 'I pray thee, then,
> Write me as one that loves his fellow-men.'
> The angel wrote, and vanished. The next night
> He came again with great awakening light,
> And showed the names whom love of God had blest;
> And, lo, Ben Adhem's name led all the rest!"

VII.

GASHMU.

Neh. vi. 6: "It is reported among the heathen, and Gashmu saith it."

My text centres in some human interests that were painfully real twenty-two hundred years ago; and I propose, first, to tell you those parts of the story that especially touch the text, and second, to note for you how the text again touches our life and time.

Nehemiah was cup-bearer to an old Persian king. The position was one of great trust. He was a Jew, a prince of the old line, whose father had preferred Persia to Palestine, and remained there when a great many of his countrymen went out of the captivity to the fatherland. It is no matter what his reasons were for settling, but I suppose he never quite forgot the old country,—no man ever does,— and contrived to transmit the love to his son, who one day happened on some Jews, fresh from Jerusalem, who told him that the people there were in very great distress; the whole province was in affliction; the walls of the city broken down, the gates burned with fire; and he tells us when he heard these things he sat down and wept and mourned, and besought God to help him get things righted. Then he determined to appeal to the king, but had to wait four months for the right moment. One day he had to give the king wine; he was very much troubled: the king saw by his face that he was sad, and said, "Why art thou sad? thou art not sick; this must be some heart sorrow." Then he said, "O king, why should I not be sad, when the city, the place of the graves of my fathers, lieth waste, and the gates are burned with fire." Then the king said, "What is thy request?" And I said unto the king, "Send me to the city of my fathers' sepulchres, that I may build it." So the king said, "How long wilt thou be gone?" And I set a time; and the king sent me away, and gave me letters to the governor to pass me on to Judah, and a letter to the chief forester, bidding him give me all the timber I wanted.

The good patriot in good time got to Jerusalem, and found about the place a party with some power, not only content to see this ruin, but determined to cry down reform; and it grieved them exceedingly that there was come a man to seek the welfare of the children of Israel. There is then a touching picture of three days silence, in which, no doubt, he pondered what had best be done. Then he rose up in the night, and with one horse and a few men made a secret survey of the ground, from the valley gate to the dragon well, from the dragon well to the fountain gate; then to the king's pool, where the ruin was so bad his horse could not get along at all. Then he went in the night by the brook, and viewed the wall, and turned back and entered the gate of the valley, and so returned; telling neither priests, nor rulers, nor nobles what he had done. And then, when all was ready, he said, "See, now, what distress we are in! let us build up the walls of Jerusalem, and take away the reproach." And I told them how the hand of God was upon me, and told them the king's words. Then they all said, "Let us rise up and build." So one party built to the sheep gate, and another to the fish gate, and one to the old gate, and one to the palace gate, and one to the valley gate, and one to the fountain gate, and one to the sepulchres, and one to the armory, and one to the horse gate. And the goldsmiths did a piece, and the apothecaries a piece, and the ministers a piece; and one man, whose children have spread over all the earth, repaired a little piece that stood just opposite his own chamber; and one family, whose children are not all lost, thank God, built a thousand cubits. So, on the twenty-fifth day of the month Elul, early in our September, fifty-two days from the time they began, walls and gates and locks and bars were all done.

But if this earnest, silent man had done no more than simply build the walls of his native city, I should not select him from ten thousand who have done as well or better. The real thing is, with him as it is with all of us, what he built with the wall; what he went through to build it; what the devil, in different forms, did to stop him, and how he kept on finding new sources of power for the exigencies of the time, holding fast steadily to God until his work was done. That is the jewel in this setting of the Scriptures that brings the man and his lesson near to you and me.

Three men especially in the community, were determined to oppose all attempts at renovation. They said it was rank rebellion against the king. They cried out, "What are these feeble Jews doing? Will they fortify themselves? Will they right things in a day? Will they create good stones out of burnt rubbish? Why, if a fox go up, he will break down their wall. If they go to do this work, rather than let them, we will surprise and kill them." But this man said, "The God of heaven will prosper us, and so we will build." And the people had a mind to work. So they prayed to God, and set a watch; and he said, "Do not be afraid, but fight for your homes, and brothers, and sons, and wives, and daughters." So some builded the wall, and some held the spears and shields; and every builder had a sword girded on his side, and he says, "I set men to blow the trumpet, so that wherever the trumpet sounded, the people should be ready to fight." So we builded and were ready to fight, and from the time when we began until we ended, from morning to starlight, and from starlight to morning, we were working and watching, and not one of us put off our garments except for the washing.

Then, when the wall was builded in the face of this enmity, when there was no hope for force, they tried fraud. They sent four times to ask this great worker to come into council, and four times he replied, "I am doing a great work, so that I cannot come down; why should the work cease, while I leave it, and come to you?" Then one of them sent his servant, with an open letter in his hand, in which was written, "It is reported among the heathen, and Gashmu saith it, that thou art intending to rebel, and hast built the wall so that thou mayest be a king, and hast set preachers in Jerusalem to proclaim thee king. Now, we will report all this to the court. Come, if thou wilt not confer with us, and let us take counsel." Then he says, I sent to them, saying, "There is no such thing done. Ye are making it out of your own heart, to stop the good work." Finally, a man came, as he claimed, from the Lord, and said, "Go into the temple, and shut thyself in to save thy life, for they mean to kill thee in the night." But I said, " Shall such a man as I flee into the temple to save my life? Where is the man that would do that? I will not go in." And when I had said that, I saw the Lord had not sent him. So the wall was finished. My text then touches, as you see, one of the most trying sorts of hinderance that every man must face and conquer, who determines to do anything ahead of the littleness and unfaithfulness of the time. And now I will note, —

I. Who Gashmu was.
II. What he tried to do; and,
III. What came of it.

I. Personally, we do not know Gashmu from the ten thousand men of his era. He was Gashmu the Arabian, and that is all.

But his real identity is not centred on the year of his birth, or who was his father, or how much he was worth, but on what he did. When our life begins, our name is almost everything; but when our life is ended, it has been heavily freighted with good or evil, and is what the things are to which it gives personal identity. This man's house has crumbled into ruin. His father, his birthday, and his money at interest have all gone into a night, for which there is no morning. The woman that loved him, the children that were born to him, the men that fought him or flattered him, have not left even a shadow on the face of the earth. What church he went to, what creed he held to, what book was most sacred to him, what ideas in politics, or morals, or religion, were final and unquestionable — these things have all gone, and left no more trace of the man than the particular flowers he tended under that September sun. But he did one solid thing; he came out square against a man who was determined to do good, and was earnestly doing it, and tried to put him down. Gashmu, I suppose, was a man whose word went a good way in that little corner of the world; a man worth referring to when you wanted to make a thing go. If he said it was so, there was no more to be said. A man who had paid his way, and kept a good name, and never disturbed his neighborhood with visionary projects, and never, up to that time, let them see that he was ignorant, or stupid, or shallow. Perhaps he did not even know it himself; or, it may be, that he was not stupid, but only selfish, or a bigot, and here was the fire to the dry wood that had been piled ready; here the one reason why he should cry, " Lead us not into temptation;" here the sin that so easily beat him.

He might have satisfied himself in half an hour that this man was all right; half an hour's talk would have convinced him that Nehemiah was an estimable, truthful, and unselfish man as ever lived. Gashmu was probably on the wrong side at the start, and was too proud to acknowledge it; or he did not like Nehemiah the first time he saw him; or had lived so long beside the ruins that he had come to admire them more than sound walls; — how can I tell you what were the motive powers that pushed him on to sin, when I see all these reasons, and a score of others, actuating the Gashmus of to-day. A motive power there must have been, but that is lost with all that he had or was. This only, this one thing is left: A good man was doing a good work with all his might, and bad men tried to hinder him. They tried to hurt his person. Gashmu was above that. He was none of your common rowdies. Sanballat and Tobiah might do that, but not Gashmu; yet Gashmu will sit there and muse his dislike, and be glad to hear the petty stories that float like thistle-down through the neighborhood against the innocent man; words are twisted and turned to meanings Nehemiah never thought of, and Gashmu hopes they are true; he wishes they were true; the wish is the father to the thought, and he believes them. One story, in particular, gets credence. This man means to be a king. I suppose at first it was only, "I wonder if he does not mean to be a king." Then "I guess he does mean to be a king." Gashmu hears the floating absurdity. On any other subject he would pronounce anything so empty as this rumor silly; but when this man is the subject of the rumor, he would rather believe it than not. He will go over the first thing to-morrow and take a look at things, not at the man, but at the walls. Then the whole bad nature of him is stirred to its uttermost deep.

There can be no reason short of rebellion to justify such a work as that; he has no doubt in his own mind now about the rebellion; he remembers twenty instances in which men have prepared for rebellion in exactly the same way;

this man certainly means to rebel. But so far Gashmu is free from the last penalty; he can go home and be silent, and he will be saved from the shame of all the ages. No, he cannot do that, for as he goes home, ready ears listen, and the fatal word is uttered in his vexation, "That man certainly means to be a king;" and he can never get that word back again, though he weep tears of blood for it. Before night it is repeated by twenty tongues, "He intends to rebel: Gashmu says it." So Gashmu has permitted his prejudices to grow into a lie. Gashmu is to live thousands of years for one purely false assertion, and to be the representative man of unprincipled gossips and narrow bigots as long as the world stands.

He cannot kill the shame; no! nor by living can he live it down. The days have grown to weeks, the weeks to months, the months to years, the years to ages, and that is still a sad name, branded with a lie. "It is commonly reported, and Gashmu said it." Note now, I pray you, some Gashmus in our churches, and our social and national life. First of all, there are Gashmus in the church, and Gashmu said it, is at the bottom of nine tenths of all the differences in Christendom.

I suppose that men will forever prefer this or that form of religion, as the Switzer prefers a mountain and the Hollander a flat. They were born to it. The first Switzer had the preference for mountains strong in his nature, and it has rooted itself deeper into every new age. So it is in the things which are, as it were, outside vital religion in all churches. The Hollander can live in Switzerland, and the Switzer in Holland, but not so well or so happily it may be; still, the fact that they can live a stout life when they change places, is conclusive on the vital life there is in both countries for both men. So it is in churches.

Some men like their religion, as the eagle likes his nest, on a bare crag above the reach of the fowler, commanding great sweeps of country and utterly alone; and some, like the lark, will soar while they sing, but build a nest on the sward with all common and lowly things that stay on the earth; and if we could ever grow so large-hearted as to recognize this spiritual conformation, it would trouble us no more to see a good man in the church of Rome than it troubles the eagle to see the lark. It would be as natural and beautiful for us to see men in the Presbyterian church, or in the Episcopalian, as it is to see one bird build in a thorn bush, another in an apple tree, and a third in a three century pine, or to see a Switzer at Berne, and a Hollander in Rotterdam. But it is notorious that this is not so. If you push the good Baptist brother to the last result of his creed, you are pretty sure to find that he can only give you the choice of very cold water, or something exactly at the other point of the diameter. The Unitarian can be logical, only in showing that Trinitarians are idolaters. Then we are as far apart as Mount Gerizim and Mount Zion were in the old time. The Jews had no dealings with the Samaritans; the Episcopalians have none with the Presbyterians, and if the members of both were not far better than the set Gashmuisms of their churches, they would be obliged to count the pastors of the Unitarian churches very wicked men.

Now, who is accountable for all this? Gashmu. It is commonly reported, and Gashmu said it. These men and women have natures as tolerant as Hollander and Switzer to swamp and mountain. They love each other heartily, and will laugh or weep for the same gladness or gloom.

They will stand at the same death-bed, and look upward in the same conviction that heaven lies above us, and pass round the same little child with the same original and beautiful untruthfulness about its perfect beauty and parental resemblance, and as long as they keep the good sweet nature, be interested alike in all these wonderful revelations to youth and maiden, which are just as fresh while the world grows older, as was the first snow-drop in Eden. But watch us when we come near the confines of creeds; just as we grow tolerant here, we are counted out as backsliders; let us be large-hearted here, and we become suspected. Who has sundered us? Gashmu. Away back in the old time, a man came, no matter whether he belonged to this church or that, saw the walls of Zion broken down and in ruins, was smitten to the heart, won men over to help him, turned to with all his might and began to repair the waste places, but Gashmu, who had got to consider the ruin just about what he wanted, got a grain of bitterness into his soul, —

> "One little pitted speck in garnered fruit,
> Which, rotting inward, slowly moulders all."

And there was uncertainty and trouble all about. The men who had lived there all their life, and were contented with the ruin, could not tell what this renovation meant. Then reports got about of designs upon the authority of the king; but it was Gashmu who made the mischief a finality. He was the man who knew most; the man the rest trusted to find out what these men were about. He did not go to the reformer and ask to see his charter. He took counsel with his own prejudice and preference, and made that his foundation, and said, This is rebellion, without the shadow of a doubt, and he is the man who made the gap. Gashmu said it, and we believe Gashmu rather than the holiest whispers of our own natures, and stand apart in that which, above all things, should bring us together. We say it is all wrong for the Switzer to prefer the mountain, or the Hollander the marsh, or the eagle the cliff, or the skylark the sod; "we distort our nature ever for our work, and count our right hands stronger for being hoofs." We forget that,

> "When all is tried, all done, all counted here,
>   All creeds, sects, churches, all philosophies,
>   That Love just puts his hand out in a dream,
>   And straight outreaches all things."

In the churches, no doubt, we should all be nearer and sweeter in Christian intercourse but for this Gashmu, who goes about blinking here and there at other sects, and asserting that what may be so, is so; and Gashmu said it, seals many an opening fountain of sweet Christian refreshing, fastens ingenuous young souls into a rigid intolerance, and builds fences between Christian men so high, that it is hopeless trying to get over.

So again in our social life, Gashmu is the curbstone where all the mischief is finally unloaded. Little rumors of no moment, the tiny sparks that are struck off in the quick, hearty friction of the daily life, need Gashmu to blow them into smoke and fire. Alone, they would die out the moment they were struck, but when they strike Gashmu, there is no dying. If it is commonly reported, and Gashmu said it, it takes a strong decision to say, the moment we hear it, "That's a lie." Your social Gashmu means well on his own estimate of things, too; his main faults are narrowness and hastiness, and a strong tendency to measure all men by his own personal standard. Perhaps he is, on the whole, a good man; lives a life that wins the respect of a whole town; tells the truth so constantly that his word is as good as gold. But some one man does not train with him; he does not like that man at all; does not understand him; and so cultivates a little feeling of dislike, until it bulges into a receptiveness of idle rumors, that would be like mere straws if they were reported of a man he loves. Yet he will nurse them, and cherish them, and at some moment his dislike will come to a head, and he will say, "I have no doubt it is true." Then Gashmu said it, clips that man's margin at the bank, draws the sunshine out of half the faces he meets on the street, and puts him in a position that, it may be, brings the very tendencies for which Gashmu has spotted him; for, "being observed where observation is not sympathy, is just being tortured." How many grown men and women regret bitterly to-day some such misjudgment on another, — the hasty word of a single moment, that we could never recall and never atone for, by which the life of the man or woman about whom we said it has been darkened and injured past redemption. It was a small matter of itself, but Gashmu said it, and that was like sowing the thing in black prairie loam, insuring to us a harvest of bitter regrets, and to our victim a harvest of bitter memories.

Then we have Gashmus in the nation and the public life; and Gashmu said it, is the most certain seven-barrelled Springfield repeater that the devil has in his whole armory. But I warn you here against believing that this Gashmu of the old heathen world is only to be found on the one side. It is impossible to study the course of public life, and not conclude that he is on all sides of all public questions, and is about as mischievous on one side as another. Gashmu is never the man that looks into things, and then takes his side and stands to it for conscience' sake; but the man who speaks out of his narrow heart and mind the lie he wants to be true, and wants others to believe. I suppose, while there is a free and healthy government in this or any other country, there will be conservatism and radicalism; a party that will hold on, as long as it can, to things as they are, and a party that will want to go ahead and reform them. And, standing as I have always done, from pure choice, with radicals, I would still try to see the good there is in conservatism, and to respect men who stand by this conviction, pleading that we shall not pull down the old house, however rickety and inconvenient it may be, before we are able to build a new one. Let the conservative stand up for time-honored, and by that I never mean time-execrated, institutions and charters, and he deserves as well of his country as any other man who will make sacrifices for her, and defend and help her to the best of his power.

But in doing this on any side, one great trouble still is Gashmu. I will venture to say there is not a faithful man in politics to-day who has only the good of the nation at heart, and so will only go with his party when his party is right, who is not constantly tormented by Gashmu. One day he will slide a paragraph into a letter from the Capitol, another day he will put a barbed arrow into the shape of a local. Then you shall find him lurking in a leader, or in a speech in Congress. Gashmu in the nation breaks out everywhere, and if God did not intend to save us as a nation with a great salvation, to make our walls strong and sure in spite of him, and all that go in his company, Gashmu would be our ruin.

Now for all this there is the concluding admonition and encouragement. And this, first of all, is clear: with all his power and prestige, Gashmu came to nothing before this earnest steady builder of waste places, and found that Gashmu said it, was no more avail to stop the building, than a pewter spoon would have been to carry it on. It was common rumor and Gashmu on the one side, and God and the right on the other; and, alas for Gashmu, when he is found fighting against God!

And so I would say to every earnest man and woman, keep true to your task, whatever it be, make your work as good as you can, put all you have into it, stand steadily by it, and never mind Gashmu. He may annoy you, he cannot hurt you; he may hinder you, he cannot stop you. It is no matter what you may be doing, — if you are faithfully at work, trying to do good, there will be a Gashmu somewhere, who will say what he can against you. All you can do, and all you have to do, is to work on silently, and trust to God, and never mind Gashmu.

Secondly, when Gashmu comes, and begins to say this and that to annoy you, do not come down to talk to him. If he wants to revile you, let him; the day will be sure to declare which is right. Common report may say wheat is chaff, and Gashmu may confirm it, as he did about this honest Hebrew. But when the wheat is once cast into the ground, and the kindly earth folds it to her breast, and the sweet rains drop down from heaven upon it, and the sun wakens all the pulses of the summer about it, then you will see, "first the blade, then the ear, and after that the full corn," and God will be true and Gashmu a liar.

Then, if you come across Gashmu in the church, or in society, or in any way whatever, keep out of his way as much as you can — have nothing to say to him. There are plenty of men and women, wherever you go, who will be glad to meet you and tell the truth, and let other people alone; who will respect your nature in religion, and your character in life, and will never think to do the truth good service by a lie; who will say to you, the church in which you can get and do the most good, is the best church, whatever be its name. No church can satisfy all. Gashmu has no more right to interfere with the church you shall go to than he has to interfere with the state you shall go to. And I venture to say that when this is once accepted generally, in the church and out of it, Gashmu will be voted a nuisance, and put down.

Then let us take care that we are not as Gashmu. It is one of the most subtle and dangerous sins I know of. I do not know of any profession that is not guilty. Gashmus among ministers, merchants, lawyers, doctors, mechanics, and men generally, and women, too, are plenty as blackberries. I have seen him in all sorts of social parties. I have even imagined I detected him in the church meeting. The danger is, he is so plausible, and seems so right, so concerned for the good of Zion, that, like the old giant in the Pilgrim's Progress, he spoils young pilgrims with sophistry. Let all young pilgrims look out lest they fall into his snare, and become like him in his vile calling; and let them watch what weight there is to the word he says about the man or the thing he dislikes, for to be like Gashmu is to be one of the most pitiful and paltry of men.

Finally, we must pity Gashmu; for, after all,

like all men who do wrong, he was finally the greater sufferer. There was, on that September morning, for all we know, a decent man who might rest, when his little life was ended, as quietly as his fathers were resting in the old Assyrian hills. Yet before nightfall he had said a few words that have impaled him on the lonely peak of twenty-two centuries, in an awful solitude, of warning to every man who will not consider the eternal sacredness of the words he may be saying about another, and their long and deep duration.

He told a lie, in his narrow prejudice, against a good man who was doing a good work for his country, his church, and his race, and now he can never rest. The Bible, that chains him fast to this everlasting damnation, has been sometimes almost lost out of the world, buried in seclusion, hidden in mountains, and caves, and dens. It has been found again, printed, translated into every tongue, and is read to-day, as the earth wheels round the sun, by untold millions of men and women. Wherever one holds a Bible, he can get at this story, how Gashmu lied when he could have told the truth, and is convicted before all the ages and all the angels; is the real Wandering

Jew unable to die. Need I say, then, do not try to be avenged on Gashmu. Vengeance is mine, saith the Lord; I will repay. Surely there is no man who will not rest his course with God after such an example as this, and instead of the bitterness we all feel when we are so wronged by Gashmu, pity the hapless fate of the wrong-doers, and cry, as one cried who was wronged as we never can be, — "Father, forgive them; they know not what they do."

VIII.

STORMING HEAVEN.

Luke xi. 5–10: "And he said unto them, Which of you shall have a friend, and shall go unto him at midnight, and say unto him, Friend, lend me three loaves; for a friend of mine in his journey is come to me, and I have nothing to set before him? And he from within shall answer and say, Trouble me not; the door is now shut, and my children are with me in bed; I cannot rise and give thee. I say unto you, Though he will not rise and give him, because he is his friend, yet because of his importunity he will rise and give him as many as he needeth. And I say unto you, Ask, and it shall be given you; seek, and ye shall find; knock, and it shall be opened unto you. For every one that asketh, receiveth; and he that seeketh, findeth; and to him that knocketh, it shall be opened."

THE text, in connection with what precedes it, seems singular. When Jesus had been praying in a certain place, his disciples came to him, and said, "Lord, teach us to pray;" and he taught them the Lord's Prayer. But when he had done this, he goes on to speak to them in a parable that seems to cast a new light on some of these relations of man to God that are to be affected through this mysterious agency. For, instead of representing the divine nature as so open and tremulous to our cry that it needs not even a whisper when we pray, but can hear our sighing and be stirred by our longing, it is opened to us here as if wrapped in a slumber heavy as midnight, and only to be awakened by our persistent and most urgent endeavor.

In all the words of the Messiah which we possess, there is but one other parable touching the same principle. It is where the widow comes, in her helplessness, to the unjust judge, who neither fears God nor regards man, and cries, "Avenge me of mine adversary." He has no mind to listen to her cry; she is the embodiment of all helplessness; there is no eloquence in her words, no gift in her hands, and no reason in the world why he should attend to her, except her simple persistence in urging her claim; but that carries the day against every obstacle. Her continual cry for what she has a right to seek has in it a touch of omnipotence; so he gives that to importunity he would not give as a duty or a right.

The first feeling we have about the matter is, either that there has been some mistake in the way these parables are reported, or that it is hopeless for us to try to understand them. We say, this householder asleep at midnight! What can this mean? I think the meaning is, that Jesus would teach us in this way what we are learning in many other ways — that the best things in the divine life, as in the natural, will not come to us merely for the asking; that true prayer is the whole strength of the whole man going out after his needs, and the real secret of getting what you want in heaven, as on earth, lies in the fact that you give your whole heart for it, or you cannot adequately value it when you get it. So, "Ask, and it shall be given you; seek, and you shall find; knock, and it shall be opened unto you," means, Put out all your energies, as if you had to waken heaven out of a midnight slumber, or an indifference like that of the unjust judge.

This I conceive to have been the meaning of Christ in the parable; and it touches something in our life we seldom adequately consider, namely, what I would call the indifference of God to anything less than the best there is in man — the determination of Heaven, if I may say so, not to hear what we are not determined Heaven shall hear. So calling out the faculty that lies hidden in our nature, to answer to another deep word of this great Teacher, "The kingdom of heaven suffereth violence, and the violent take it by force;" and any adequate answer to our cry of, "Let thy kingdom come," must greatly lie in our power to bring in the kingdom.

We can see this principle at work, if we will, first in nature. It fills the whole distance between the paradise of the first pair and this common earth as we find it to-day. In that old Eden, there was no barrier between the longing and its answer, and no effort needed to bring the answer, except the longing. The kindly, easy, effortless life went on, we suppose, as life might have gone on in the Sandwich Islands before Cook discovered them, had their inhabitants possessed the secret of how to live, in addition to their perfect climate, and the daily bread that came almost without the asking.

In this life of ours, however, there is no such answer to our natural cry for what we need. The need may be, in its way, divine, and the longing as divine as the need; but before they can come to their full fruition, barriers have to be broken down that seem to have been put there by Heaven itself. There is always a divine inertness and hinderance to be overcome before we can come to what is more divine than that which we possess.

I can remember nothing in my childhood, for instance, of a deeper interest than the stories I used to read of hapless travellers crossing the Alps, and being overtaken by the storm and lost, of their rescue by the great sagacious dogs and their masters, and their restoration to life; and the old interest was still so strong in 1865, that when I came to the foot of one of the great passes which I had no time to cross, I lingered about it with an almost tireless interest.

But I went to see also the new railroad they are making by a tunnel through Mount Cenis, that shall do away forever with the hardship and danger of the passes over the mountains, and open up a new and living way between Switzerland and Italy. And there I caught, I think, the first hint of this barrier thrown up by Heaven across its own highways. For in spite of the bemoanings of Mr. Ruskin about desecrating the holy shrines of these lakes and mountains with the scream of the locomotive, and the careless tread of the multitude on their cheap trip, I can imagine no comparison between such a road and the old track over their crests that does not prove the railroad the more heavenly way, in safety to life, in salvation from suffering, in economy of time, in closeness of intercourse, in facility for seeing whatever is most glorious on either side, in opening the pages of that poem of the world to the million, that until now has been closed to all but the few. The railroad is beyond all comparison the better and diviner way.

But the moment the nations began to long for such a road, the barriers against it began to appear. The earth is the Lord's, and he made it; but for such a railroad he made no provision beyond this, — that no man can touch or weigh or measure the determination of some men that there shall be one. "Let us have a railroad," they say; and then they go to work, with the geometries that are a part of the order of the universe, to find the way. They trace it along the old natural levels, and it would seem as if they were made to be an answer to this prayer; but then at last they come to the mountain, to the great inert divine hinderance, as immovable as the midnight slumber on the unwilling heart. "We want a railroad into Italy," cries the world, "and can go no farther for this mountain. What shall we do to find a way?" "There is no way," Heaven answers, "except to your persistency; but if you seek, you shall find; if you knock, it shall be opened to you." And so the seeking of the answer to that prayer of the nations is intrusted to the keen sight of men whose searching will never tire until the way is found. The knocking is with hard steel at the hard rock, and it is only a question of persistence and of endurance; then at last it has come to pass that even the heart of the unwilling mountain is won, and its midnight sleep driven away; and where for countless ages there has been only an utter and unutterable silence, there is now the mighty response of an answered prayer in the thunder of the locomotive.

We touch this principle again in a more personal way when we observe this striving in the experiences of men. Not to mention at this moment what is most purely spiritual in these conflicts, there is deep instruction in watching how some man is moved to do some thing that is to bless the world in a new and wonderful way when it is done; but between the conception and the conclusion there are mighty barriers, that only the uttermost might of what is indeed a divine persistence can finally overcome. It flashes on the soul with something of the nature of a revelation when it is done. Men say he must have been inspired to do it. Its blessing is so clear that we can almost see the shining track on which it has come from God to man. It would be natural to think then the way must be clear between the conception and execution of such a thing, not only because of the nobility of the thing itself, but of the urgent need of it among men. Yet the new child is still laid in the manger, and has to struggle in the long lapse between the birth and the baptism through the hinderance of its Nazareth, while the world must wait and want until all the barriers in the way of its coming are broken down.

How strikingly — to take what is right at our

hand — this has been brought home to us in the wonderful history of the perfecting of India-rubber! Delicately winning its way into the most essential arts and uses of life, no mean agent in our new civilization, so indispensable is it, now we have learned its use, that if it should be suddenly taken away, it would leave a great gap in our commonwealth, and shorten the averages of human life. I know of nothing more impressive in the line of my thought than that long prayer, as I must call it, of the inventor, by which at last he won the unlistening heavens over to his side. With a faith in the thing he wanted to do, teachers of religion might well imitate; with as little care for the mere wealth that might come of his discovery as a man could well feel; consecrating every power and every penny he could command to the one great purpose; counted a madman by the sensible, easy-going world about him, that could neither feel the burden of his soul, nor win its reward,—the story of the way in which he persisted, year after year, in broken health and utter poverty, and what was worse than starvation for himself, in wrestling with the silent and seemingly dumb heavens for their revelations, is one of the most touching things in the history of our human life.

There was the blessing all the time hidden in the heart of Providence. What the thing is now with us, we cannot but believe it was then with God. But what the world believed in old time, as it dwelt within the shadows of a cruel superstition, still comes true to us, as we dwell in the clear daylight of the divine law,—that when a man will win some mighty blessing for his fellow-men, the blessing can only come at the cost of his most precious blood: he must not grow weary; he must weary that which holds the secret. Let him give up his search too soon, let him knock too seldom, the householder will not rise; the bread will not be given. The only comfort there is,—and it is the only one we need,—is this, that when once a man casts his whole manhood into the thing God has stirred him up to seek, he never does knock too often; but if he must, he dies knocking, and then leaves another at the door.

They knocked more than two hundred years for the locomotive before the door was opened, and if you have read this history of Mr. Goodyear, to which I have referred, you will remember how at last the full revelation of the secret came in a flash, as when the diamond seeker watches for the sudden sheen of his treasure between the sand and the sun. But it was the eye that had been seeking patiently, persistently, and steadily through these long years that found the treasure, as when the apple fell; if we had been there, we should have seen an apple fall where Newton saw the whole order of the suns and stars, because he had been wearying heaven night and day for years to open her doors to his beseeching about that matter.

And if we leave these semi-material things, and consider what is, perhaps, more purely in the line of the parable, it is only to see still more certainly how certain is this matter of the unlistening ear and unwilling heart of Providence in the experiences of the noblest and best. The whole history of man, in his higher relations to God, is the history of a struggle through the most disheartening and perplexing hinderances into the light and life in which the soul so led can break the bread of life to others. The truth the man has to tell, he has first to win at a cost which leaves nothing else of any worth by comparison, and then his very life is cheerfully given, if need be, rather than the truth shall fail.

I will venture to say, there is not a supreme man of God, in any time, or race, or religion, whose power may not be understood better by this test than by any other we can find; sent into the world, with the purpose he finally fulfils folded within his soul; inspired from above to enter on his work; sealed when his work is done, and set fast forever among the prophets and apostles of the race, you shall always find that there is a time stretching often over a long span of years in which the man had to strive and pray, to weary Heaven by his incessant beseeching, until at last, perhaps, when it became a question with those who were aware of the contest, whether Heaven should hear or the man should die, the heart of the great secret is won, the angel says, " Thou shalt be called no longer Jacob, but Israel, because thou hast wrestled with God and prevailed; " and then, in the strength of his well-won blessing, he is forever after set among the great ones of the world.

But the truth was as true before the man was born, as it is when he is like to die in his struggle to pluck it out of the silence in which it is hidden. Descartes and Kepler did not set the heavens in the order they almost died to discover; justification by faith was as true when Luther was singing his Christmas hymns as when he was worn away with the misery of his crying, "How shall man be just with God?" The loaves are there; the whole secret is in the winning, and in why they have to be so won, as the hills and valleys of Canaan were standing in the clear sunshine through all that forty years Israel was wading wearily through the desert towards them.

So, then, we come, through these illustrations of this principle in our life, to some lessons which we shall all do well to learn; and I cannot mention one before this: that instead of a prayer being something we can say easily at any time and be done with, can read out of a book, or have said for us by a minister, — in the most sacred and essential sense, a true prayer must be the deepest and most painful thing a man can possibly do; may be so costly that he will give up, without a murmur, his very life, before he will give up that which his prayer has wrested, as it were, out of the heart of the heavens; and it may be so protracted, that twenty years shall not suffice to say it.

For prayer, in its purest reality, is first the cry of the soul to God for his gift, and then it is the effort of the soul to make as sure of what it longs for, as if it were to come by its own winning. It is something in which the words we say are often of the smallest possible consequence, and only our unconquerable persistence under God is omnipotent. And that this longing and striving, as shadowed out in the parable, should be so painful and protracted, is only a wonder when we lose sight of the revelations made to us in almost every other direction.

I went once to see the Cathedral at Cologne. It is the most wonderful blossoming of Gothic art on the planet. Hundreds of years ago some man, now forgotten, found it all in his heart, and longed to make it visible in stone. But because it was so great and good, when the man died his work was still unfinished; it was still unfinished when his name was forgotten; at last, even the design of it was lost, and it seemed as if there was no hope that the Cathedral would ever be done. But when Napoleon went storming through Europe, his marshals lighted on the old design, hidden in some dusty corner of a monastery; so it got back again to Cologne, and when I was there, all Germany was interested in finishing the noble idea.

Now, since that church was begun, thousands of churches have risen and fallen in Germany, and no trace of them is left; but because the Dome Kirch is the grandest thing in its way that was ever done in stone, or ever conceived in a soul, two things follow: there must be a mighty span between the conception and the consummation, a striving through dark days and fearful hinderances to build it, and, at the same time, an indestructible vitality in the idea, like that which has attended it. It is but a shadow of this great fact concerning our spiritual life. The very worth of what we ask for from the heavens, because it is so worthy, is the deepest reason there is why the blessing cannot come until the full time — until it has had its own time.

It is, therefore, no reason why a man earnestly engaged in a true reform in the ideas or the conduct of life, should become disheartened, and think of giving up, when the thing, being in his opinion a matter of such supreme importance to mankind, and so verily a truth of God, does not win its way more rapidly or receive more open marks of the divine favor, but has to labor under every possible disadvantage, and be as if the heart of Heaven was unwilling to recognize its claim. It is probable that in exact proportion to the worth of the thing will be the strife for the place it must finally take, and the work it must finally do; and this, not that Heaven is on the other side or indifferent, but it will make full proof of those who are to be intrusted with the mighty interest, and make the worth of the interest clear.

And so the principle I have noticed in the life of the reformer, is to be noticed also of every great reform: it has to wait, and work its way persistently through the most determined opposition; through times in which there is no encouragement at all, except that which is in the hearts of those who are devoted to it, who know right well if they ask, and seek, and knock, and do not tire, but keep right on, then, as sure as there is an eternal right, the wrong will be at last conquered, and Heaven will be won to give what they shall not be weary asking. Then, for reform and reformer alike, will come the answer to the prayer of the old apostle, "The God of all grace, who hath called you unto his eternal glory after that ye have suffered awhile, establish, strengthen, settle you, and make you perfect."

And so it must be with those reforms in which we take an interest in these days: the reform in religious ideas, by which we are all at last to come to the unity of spirit in the bond of peace; to one Lord, one faith, and one baptism: or the woman question, in which simple natural justice will take the place of the prescriptions and miserable unfairness of the old ages: or intemperance, in which the commonwealth is not now ashamed to be implicated in licensing what works more ruin than every other course of which we have any knowledge: or this labor question, in which, as yet, the one side is tyrant now, and then the other, and each seeks only its own; as if the relation between man and man was a great tumor of human selfishness. These and all other questions assuming in these days a vital importance are touched by the parable. In the long span that they must take between the conception and the consummation, Heaven will seem to be dead to the cry of those that hold them in their hearts; but they can be sure, as if victory had crowned their banners, that when the full time has come, then will come the full answer to their cry, and not one grain of what is locked fast in God's truth and righteousness of the thing they strive for can ever be lost out of the good endeavor.

So, once more, when we remember that this life each man and woman is living, is to the liver by far the most precious thing he can have to do with; how its experiences, lessons, and results enter into the very substance of the soul; we must not wonder if some things we have at heart do not come to pass so readily as we may think they ought, being so surely the gift of Heaven, but lag and linger after all our longing, and the endeavor which is in itself a prayer, as if Heaven is determined indeed we shall not have them, or is deaf to our cry. It is possible in the light of the lessons I have tried to draw, not from the parable alone, but from the deep and constant facts of life that come up and range themselves about the parable, that the very magnitude and worth of the thing we want may be the reason why it is delayed, as well as that the things which come into our possession in waiting for it and striving for it, are quite as good to have and to hold as the thing itself.

The young man strives for what we call success in life; by which we mean, too often, money enough to be independent of any of those surprises of a good Providence which always fall to the lot of the poor, earnest, struggling man, and a position in which he can stand, as nearly as possible, like to the golden image the king set up in the plains of Dura. But let it be a real success the young man aims at — the success of being most useful and powerful for good; the thing he seeks may still be delayed by its very magnitude and excellence.

There is a fine illustration of this in one notable family that sprang up not far from the place where I was born. Long ago the fore-elders were small farmers, but four generations back the man of that time began to feel after a better place — to knock at the door of heaven for a rise. When he died he had a little spinning interest and a well-grown son who built up, bit by bit, through a long life and many hard fortunes, the idea he had derived from his father. In the third generation the effort had come to be a splendid success, and in the fourth it culminated, probably, in a man who with wealth and education had a noble native power that had been growing gradually ever since that great-grandsire felt moved to knock and ask for something better than to cultivate a hungry Lancashire upland. This man in his day rendered a service to England second to none. He was

> "The statesman in the council set,
> Who knew the seasons, when to take
> Occasion by the hand, and make
> The bounds of freedom wider yet."

And so, I think, if the eldest of all, in his grim struggle to get the blessing of success — for a real, healthy success is a blessing — could have seen the youngest standing at the helm, and guiding the ship of state through some of her most dangerous passages, and then could have seen how the great qualities that made him so eminent had not come by a mere chance, but were intimately interlocked with all the good fights the whole ancestry had fought against what seemed to them often to be an inert or unwilling Providence, he would have been satisfied that this whole four-fold life, being in a deep sense also one life, should be perfected in this Sir Robert.

So, if God visits the sins, he also visits the holiness, of the fathers upon the children, unto the third and fourth generation. Let no man, therefore, striving hard to succeed, but held back by hinderance, conclude that a poor mite of this world's wealth is all that he is to get out of the endeavor. It is as certain as anything can be, that one or more of those children about his knees, who already know something of his heart-sickness, are feeling afresh the power to knock which may be failing in himself, and what he cannot give them in a banker's balance, will still come to them in a wealth that is infinitely better, — the wealth of a clear head, and a strong heart, and a divine persistence in seeking what it is his hunger and thirst to find.

My heart would be heavy, sometimes, did I not believe that my own good father, whose utmost endeavor could never carry him beyond the anvil,— at which he fell down dead from over-work many years ago,— is aware, as he abides in the rest that remains for all weary men and women, how the children for whom he cared, and wrought, and died, had come into possession of what is better than the money he could never save,— the life, good and true he lived for their sakes, and gave for their blessing.

It is to me one of the most cruel and inhuman things that is ever done, to make a man an outcast from Christian society and sympathy, who, sincerely seeking to know the truth about God, and the soul, and immortal life, still has to tell us he cannot believe it; that, after all he can do, these things are all in the dark, the doors will not open, the treasure is still hidden away, the gift of God still held back after all his knocking and cries. The time will come, as the Lord liveth, when such men and women will command the deepest sympathy and tenderness religion has to give. When, instead of the church casting them out beyond her borders, she will gather them into her very heart; will learn what this meant which her great Captain said, "The

Son of man came to seek and to save that which was lost."

It is not so now; and yet to men and women with such doubts, I say, the very magnitude and worth of the thing you are seeking may well be the deepest reason why you shall not soon find it, but shall be led still to seek, and struggle, and cry, and watch those that are satisfied, and to say, "I would give the world if I could feel as they do." It may well be that your prayer for the revelation you need will span your whole lifetime; that now and then there will be a flash, and then again the dark; yet what you come to in this seeking, is a treasure you could not come to in the finding.

> "You make the larger faith your own;
> The power is with you in the night
> That makes the darkness and the light,
> And dwells not in the light alone."

It is only and altogether essential that we shall be sure the treasure is there: that this is no delusion, which has come sweeping through human souls in floods of living light, filling them with joy unspeakable and full of glory, bringing God so near that they have instinctively called him Father; so informing them of heaven, that it never occurred to them any one could doubt it; quickening the soul so with the sense of her immortality, that she would soar and sing immortal songs out of her heart's treasure, and nerve her poor organism to meet the axe, or cross, or flame, as quietly as if it was but the pleasant prelude to her rest. You must believe, struggling, doubting, seeking, beseeching man or woman that the door opened to them will be opened to you. They found the gift you are seeking; the silent heavens heard them at last, and gave them all they sought.

Only this one thing we must never disbelieve. Let us say we cannot believe in God, or heaven, or immortality ourselves, if that indeed be the condition of our own souls. It cannot be wrong to tell the truth; and if this be the truth in our religious experience, that the householder has not risen to give us bread, it is a simple fact, and to tell it, if I feel I must, is honest and manful; but it is a wretched thing to assail that great multitude no man can number, who through all the ages have compelled Heaven to hear their cries, have eaten the bread of life and are satisfied, who do believe in God and immortality, and have left a broad, shining track that can never grow dim.

The uttermost woe that can come to a man from this direction, is not the inability he feels in himself to find these mighty confidences, but the inability to believe they have ever been found; that the householder has ever risen to give bread to any soul. It is ashes to ashes, and dust to dust, when I make my own destitution the measure of the fulness of the gospel of God. It is as foolish for me to do that, as it would be for a blind man to turn his blank orbs to the June glory, and say, "I see all there is." Let me still rest in this solid certainty, that multitudes, through all the ages, have succeeded, where I have failed; winning the bread I hunger for; finding the answer denied to my cry; the answer that I shall surely find in the fulness of time or of eternity. **Amen.**

IX.

WHY HEROD FEARED JOHN.

MARK vi. 20: "Herod feared John."

HEROD was a king; John was a subject. Herod was in a palace; John was in a prison. Herod wore a crown; John most probably did not even own a turban. Herod wore the purple; John wore camlet, as we should call it. Soldiers and servants watched the eye of Herod, and waited on his will; only the headsman waited hungrily for John. Herod came of a line that had never been famous either for morals or religion: they said, practically what a famous American long afterwards said verbally, "that religion is a very good thing in its place;" they had done their best to establish a government in which the old Jewish worship should serve as a decoy duck to the new Jewish kingdom; they made it what the State forever makes the Church when it gets a chance — a fountain of preferment, with which it can bribe or buy the upper, and a mystic spell by which it can weave fetters of superstition for the lower, classes; and up to this time the dynasty had succeeded substantially in doing what it proposed to do. Yet still "Herod feared John."

Herod, the elder, father of this Herod Antipas who feared John, was a man of notable power. Appointed over Judea by Julius Cæsar, about forty-seven years before our Christian era, he fought his way through invasion from without and treachery from within, until he had at last established the throne on what seemed, for those times, to be deep foundations. He was what one might call an Eclectic in religion. When he ascended the throne, he made offerings to Jupiter of the capitol; his coins, as well as those of his son, bear only Greek inscriptions. Yet he rebuilt the temple at Jerusalem in a style of magnificence surpassing even that of Solomon. But then he built a temple for the Samaritans, too; and, indeed, was a man full of politeness — a sort of human Pantheon, in which Greek and Roman, Jew and Samaritan, were welcome to set up their symbols, — for which he cared no more than if he himself had been so much marble; and finally, so far as we can trace him, he left his principles and his kingdom, in the full prime of their strength, to his son.

John was the son of an obscure Jewish country priest and his wife: the child of their old age. There is no hint that John had any wealth, or name, or fame, or education, or influence, when he began his life as a man. He comes on the scene as a rough, angular man, with not many words and not many friends. Herod began to reign just about when John began to live, so that there was no preponderant age in the priest's son over the king's son: that was all on the other side.

Indeed, by all mere surface facts, principles, and analogies, John ought to have feared Herod; he ought to have bated his breath and bent his head before him. John's life was not worth thirty minutes' purchase, if Herod did but give the sign to kill him. And John knew that, and Herod knew it too. Yet they rise up like ghosts before us out of that distant time — the king in the palace, the reformer in the prison; the king with the sceptre in his hand, the reformer with the shackle on his wrist. But the eye of the prisoner burns with a clear lustre, and looks right on; the eye of the king quails under its drooping lid. The hand of the prisoner is cool, and his foot firm; his head erect, and his voice clear as the voice of a trumpet. The hand of the king is hot, his step uncertain, his head bowed, and his voice broken, and, as you watch them, you get a great sense that the two men have somehow changed places — the king is a prisoner, the prisoner a king.

Now, I propose to discuss at this time the roots of this power and weakness, to see what made Herod so weak and John so strong, and to ask this question, What can we, who are set as John was, in the advance guard of reformers, do to make a deep, clear mark?

And I note for you that John had three great roots of power: First, he was a powerful man by creation — a man with a clear head, a steady nerve, and a nature set in a deadly antagonism to sin and meanness of every sort and degree. He was the Jewish John Knox, or John Brown.

> "When he saw a thing was true,
> He went to work and put it through."

He could die, but he could not back down. Now, truly, there is a sure and solid principle at the heart of these old chronicles that tell us how angels came as messengers from God to notify the world of the advent of his most glorious sons; that when God wants a particular sort of man, to do a singular work for him, at a critical time, he makes him, and sends him, angel-guarded, to his place; so that no man can be John, but John himself.

Every time I meet a man who is a man, and not a stick, I ask myself one question: "Why are you the man you are? Whence does your power hint itself to me? Whence does it come?" And while the ultimate answer has never come out of Phrenology, or Physiognomy, or any of the sciences that profess to tell you what a man is by how he looks, yet the indicative answer has always lain in that direction. In the head, and face, and form of a man there is certainly something that impresses you in some such way as the weight, color, and inscription of a coin reveal to you, with a fair certainty, whether it be gold, or silver, or — brass; and it is possible, too, that the line in which a man has descended, the country in which he is born, the climate, the scenery, the history, the poetry, and the society about him, have a great deal to do with the man.

The father, in Queen Elizabeth's time, as I have known in old English families, may be twenty-two carat gold; and the children in Queen Victoria's time may be no better than lead. That mysterious antagonism that sows tares among the wheat, sows baseness in the blood; and if there be not forever a careful and most painful dividing and burning, the tares will in time come to nearly all there is on the soil. But still forever the great mint of Providence beats on, silently, certainly, continually, sending its own new golden coins to circulate through our human life, and on each of them stamping the infallible image and superscription that tells us "this is gold." Nay, the same great Providence makes not only gold coins, but silver and iron, too; and if they are true to their ring, they are all divine; as in all great houses there be divers vessels, some to more honor and some to less honor, but not one to dishonor if it be true to its purpose; for while the golden vase that holds the wine at the feast of a king is a vessel of honor, so is the iron pot that holds the meats in the furnace; the Parian vase that you fill with flowers is a vessel of honor, and so is the tin dipper with which you fill it at the well.

For me, it is a wonderful thing to study merely the pictures of great men. There is a power in the very shadow that makes you feel they were born to be kings and priests unto God. But if you know a great man personally, you find a power in him which the picture can never give you. It is the difference between the picture of a tree and a tree, or between paste and jewels; and as you try to reach back to first principles, to search out the reason why he is what he is, — as you search for it in the sciences I have mentioned, and in family descent, and in climate, and scenery, and society,—though these all hint some truth to us, they are at the best only as the figures and pointers on the dial. Their utmost use is to mark the movement within; and that movement is worthless, if it be not chorded with the sun and stars. And so, too, I love those old, solemn, primitive affirmations that make the outward of the best men but indicative of the inward, and that again a transcript of the mind of God. So I care little for our birth and breeding, if there is this purpose of God, that we shall be genuine in our inmost nature.

I suppose this good Jewish country parson, the father of John, from the little we can glean about him, was just a gentle, timid, pious, retiring man, whose mind had never risen above the routine of his humble post in the temple; a man who would have talked for a week, or a month, or a year about some little courtesy Herod had shown him; a man devoted to the priesthood, just as the father of Franklin, in this old town of Boston, was to the making of candles, or Luther's father in Germany to the making of charcoal, or Shakespeare's to the selling of oxen at Stratford, or Johnson's of books — good, true men, iron, copper, or silver, and bidding fair to raise a family that is iron, or copper, or silver, too. But lo! God, in the full time, drops just one golden ingot down into that family treasury, pure, ponderous, solid gold; for

> "It is the growing soul within the man
> That makes the man grow:
> Just as the fiery sap the touch from God
> Careering through a tree dilates the bark,
> So life deepening within us deepens all."

Yet I need not tell you that there is a theory of human nature that busies itself forever in trying to prove that our human nature in itself is abominably and naturally despicable. Towards their fellow-men, the holders of this idea are as particular about their character and standing as the rest of us. They shall rise from their prayers, in which they have called themselves twenty hard names, and if you repeat over but one of them, instantly they are offended. Towards us, they are as particular upon points of honor as a Spaniard. Towards God, they turn with not one shred of self-respect — "they like to be despised." They insist upon it that God never cast a golden coin into this world at all — that our common human nature is nothing but base metal, with awful chances that it will ever be aught else — that if saved, then saved by transmutation — if lost, then lost because, though the Almighty considered them worth making, he did not consider them worth transmuting.

There are two replies to this theory. The first is found in that good story you have all read in a lately printed book. "Janet," said the minister, "there is really nothing in you that is at all worthy of salvation. Now, suppose God, at the last, should let you drop into hell. What would you say to that?" Janet was on her death bed. She had been all her life in this dark shadow of a possible predestination to the pit. But she had lain still in her room, in this sickness, a long time, and her soul had caught, now and again, with great distinctive vividness, a flash of the Eternal Light that at these times touches the soul from the land where the Lord God is the Sun. "Minister," Janet said, quietly, "I have thought it all over. I believe God will do with me just whatever he has a mind to do. I cannot tell what he will do. But this I know: he made me; I am the work of his hands; and if he puts me down into hell, he will lose more by doing it than I shall by bearing it." The second reply is embodied in the fact, that God does in all times and places send golden men into this world. Gold is the mine, it may be; or gold and sand and mica — gold that needs to be pounded, and melted, and purified by fire; but still, at the heart of all, real gold, — gold by creation, and not by transmutation, — needing only what it finds in God and in life to bring it out into full perfection.

Now, this primitive intrinsic nature, I say, was the first element that made John mightier in the prison than Herod was in the palace. The one was a king by creation; the other was only a king by descent. And then, secondly, there comes into the difference another element. Herod made the purple vile by his sin; John made the camel's hair radiant by his holiness. And in that personal truth, this rightwiseness, this wholeness, he gained every divine force in the universe over to his side, and left to Herod only the infernal forces. It was a question of power, reaching back ultimately, as all such questions do, to God and the devil. So the fetter was turned to a sceptre, and the sceptre to a fetter, and the soul of the Sybarite quailed, and went down before the soul of the saint.

Now this, as we enter into his spirit and life, is what comes home to us with the most invincible power and clearness. We weigh the hints of those old writers about John, and gather from them that he was intrinsically sound, from the outermost surface to the innermost centre of his life. Whatever error he might make in being hard and insensible to the beauty and glory, the more tender and lovable aspects of life, his life, as he got it, was a whole life. There are not many men in this world who begin life determined to be sinful. The set of our determination is the other way. I think God takes care that every young man shall get flashes of the beauty of holiness, and of the ghastliness of sin; and that no man will quietly determine to break away from that passable beauty, with no hope of getting back again. But a great number of young men begin to sin spasmodically. They drink the waters of sin, as the dog in Egypt is said to drink of the Nile. Being in a wholesome fear of some lurking crocodile, he just laps a little, and then runs a little, and so keeps on lapping and running, until he is either satisfied or snapped up.

Then there is a second class of men, who start in life determined to go right on, and to do just about right. And they do seem to go right on; yet still, when they themselves measure their track by long distances, there is a shadow of deflection. They are conscious of hearing a little to the left. They are not in the direct line in which they started. While no one step seems to be more than a hair's breadth out of the true line, and one earnest moment every day, one careful observation by the Eternal Sun, would put them right, yet they do not take it. It is easier sailing as it is. When the Indian, on the great prairies of the Far West, goes out to hunt the wild horse, and the horse, seeing him come, shakes his mane, and gallops with the fleetness of the wind, he never follows directly in the track of the animal he is after, for he knows it will be hopeless trying to overtake him that way. But he simply observes the almost insensible deflection of his victim from the true line, and he knows that the horse is sure to keep on that side of the line. So he crosses the arc of flight, as the string crosses the bow, with the certainty of meeting his victim at the point of attachment, though he may never see him for fifty miles. So sin and retribution are victim and victor! So the line of deflection becomes itself the guide to retribution! All day long the wrong-doer sees only the boundless landscape, and speeds along, rejoicing in the vast latitudes of freedom; but at sunset his neck is in the lasso, and he is led captive by the devil at his will.

Then the good man, the true, upright, downright man of power, goes right on to the mark. Let me tell you a story given me by the late venerable James Mott, of Philadelphia, whose uncle, fifty years ago, discovered the island in the Pacific inhabited by Adams and his companions, as you have read in the story of "The Mutiny of the Bounty." I was talking with him one day about it, and he said that, after staying at the island for some time, his uncle turned his vessel homeward, and steered directly for Boston, — sailing as he did from your own good city, — eight thousand miles distant. Month after month the brave craft ploughed through storm and shine, keeping her head ever homewards. But as she came near home, she got into a thick fog, and seemed to be sailing by guess. The captain had never sighted land from the time they started; but one night he said to the crew, " Now, boys, lay her to! I reckon Boston harbor must be just over there somewhere; but we must wait for the fog to clear up before we try to run in." And so, sure enough, when the morning sun rose it lifted the fog, and right over against them were the spires and homes of the great city of Boston! So can men go right onward over this great sea of life. The chart and compass are with them; and the power is with them to observe the meridian sun and the eternal stars. Storms will drive them, currents will drift them, dangers will beset them; they will long for more solid certainties; but by noon and by night they will drive right on, correcting deflections, resisting adverse influences, and then, at the last, when they are near home, they will know it. The darkness may be all about them, but the soul shines in its confidence; and the true mariner will say to his soul, "I will wait for the mist to rise with the new morning; I know home is just over there." Then in the morning he is satisfied; he wakes to see the golden light on temple and home. So God brings him to the desired haven.

Now John was one of those right-on men. With the sort of power, above all others, to be ruined if any suspicion of impurity could be made to cling to his name, living in a community where any handle for such suspicion would be hailed as a providence to destroy his influence, he held on in his own severely pure, strong life, from the country parsonage to the block; and the most malicious in all Jewry never whispered the possibility of a stain. Had there been a crevice in John's armor, Herod would have found it out and laughed at him; but in the presence of that pure life, that deep, conscious antagonism to sin, that masterful power, won as a soldier wins a hard battle, this man on the throne was abased before that man in the prison. Herod could muster courage to face a partial purity; but a whole man was to him what the spear of the angel was to the vile thing whispering at the ear of the first mother. It changed the possible fitness of nature into the positive deformity of hell. Therefore Herod feared John.

Then the third root of power in this great man, by which he mastered a king, — by which he became a king, — lay in the fact that he was a true, clear, unflinching, outspoken preacher of holiness. There are diverse ways of trying to reach the soul that has sunk down into sin and sensualism, as this soul of Herod had sunk. Some preachers reflect the great verities of religion, as bad boys reflect the sun from bits of broken glass. They stand just on one side, and flash a blaze of fierce light across the eyes of their victim, and leave him more bewildered and irritated than he was before. Such a one is your fitful, changing *doctrinaire*, whose ideas of right and wrong, of sin and holiness, of God and the devil, to-day, are not at all as they were last Sunday; who holds not that blessed thing, an ever-changing, because an ever-growing and ripening faith, but a mere sand-hill of bewilderment, liable to be blown anywhere by the next great storm. Then there is another sort of preacher, who is like the red light at the head of a railway night train. He is made for warning; he comes to tell of danger. That is the work of his life. When he is not doing that, he has nothing to do. I hear friends at times question whether this man has a divine mission. Surely, if there be danger to the soul, — and that question is not yet decided in the negative, — then he has to the inner life a mission as divine as that of the red lamp to the outer life. And I know myself of men who have turned sharp out of the track before his fierce glare, who, but for him, had been run down, and into a disgraceful grave. But the true preacher of holiness, the real forerunner of Christ, is the man who holds up in himself the divine truth, as a true mirror holds the light, so that whoever comes to him, will see his own character just as it is.

Such a man was this who mastered a king. His soul was never distorted by the traditions of the elders, or the habits of "good society," as it is called. On the broad clear surface of his soul, as on a pure still lake, you saw things as if in a great deep. He had no broken lights, for he held fast to his own primitive nature, and to his own direct inspiration. He did not need much lurid fire, though he used it sometimes; but he was essentially a child of the day, and realities shone when he stood near them. Men needed but to come near him, and they saw just what they were. And so, as he stood by the Jordan, crying, "Repent ye, for the kingdom of heaven is at hand," the merchant came, and went away resolving to rectify that false entry at the customs; the farmer went home and shifted the old landmark back again, so as to restore the few inches he had cribbed so cunningly the week before last; the soldier determined to pay that widow for her care; the publican said to himself, "From this time forth I will take a true tax, and no more, as the Lord liveth;" and Herod came, as the English queen came to the mirror when all her beauty was turned to ashes, and the sight was an intolerable horror to his soul, so that he could bear to look no more. Had John held only the broken lights of mere optimism before the soul of this simple king, or come to him with a message deriving its power from the last readings of the Talmud, or even the Prophets, Herod would have snapped his fingers in his face and laughed him to scorn. But there stood the man as God made him — deep, calm, pure, clear; touching in his earnest words the roots of things; saying honestly, "Herod, this deed about thy brother's wife is a piece of vileness! Thou shalt not take her!" So, though he still cleaved to his sin, Herod saw his soul as the queen saw her face scarred and netted with bad passions, and he was terrified at the vision of himself.

I tell you it is no matter what you may come to be, as the result of your true and honest life. Men may revile you, and cast you out; but through it all, if you are true to God you shall feel that there is a life of the soul that pales all other in its exceeding glory. John may be in the prison, with his poor garment of camel's hair, and with the headsman waiting for him outside; but he is blessed beyond all telling, compared with Herod in the palace, with slaves to watch his merest nod. For the one has even now breaking upon his soul the glory from that great city where the Lord God is the light; the thick walls of cloud are already lifting before the morning sun; he knows the home lies just over there. But the other has only a leap in the dark, after a life in the dark, with dark faces in the dark all about him. My friends, endure hardship like good soldiers. Ye shall reap your reward.

X.

MARRIAGE.

THE most sacred relation of humanity is that of husband and wife. They stand for more than father and mother, or parents and children, because they are the fountain from which these relations spring; and, changing the mere man and woman into these sacred names, makes that a glory which were otherwise a shame.

According to the Bible, it is a relation as old as our human history; and nothing outside of the Bible, that I know of, contradicts this testimony. Other old books cast the matter into other forms, as they themselves are the product of other races; but the whole story looks like this, when it is told, that in the beginning the divine power made man and woman, and set them on the throne of the world, and gave them from the first the grace to be husband and wife, to find in each other the counterpart and completion of their own being.

While the creation over which they were given dominion followed its special instinct, and sought its lair or made its nest, there brought forth its young, and before another spring knew them for its own no more than if they were on another continent, this husband and wife made them a home, reared a family, were steadfast not for a few months, but for a lifetime, to those that were born of their body; sent them out in due time, to do as they had done, but still counted them and their children as an intimate belonging of the old homestead; and so this human race has never evened itself with the beasts that perish, except as it has become lower and worse. It is husband and wife wherever you find them — he the weapon-man and she the web-man, as the old Anglo-Saxon Bible translates those words of Jesus, where he says, "Have ye not read that he which made them at the beginning made them male and female — he the weapon-man, she the web-man; he the defender, and she the clother; he the warrior, and she the weaver; each indispensable to the other, and both indispensable to the whole."

The divine alchemy, if I may use the word,

that transmutes the man and woman into husband and wife, is marriage. It always has been so, and no doubt always will be. The observance of marriage as a ceremony is a very different thing in different countries and times; ranging all the way from the custom of the Australian black, who beats the maiden he will take until she is insensible, and then carries her off to his hut, to the pure and simple ceremonial used in the best Protestant communions. In the grossest savagery, marriage is, as a rule, as rude and brutal as possible. As we rise in the true scale of life it takes a nobler and better form, and on the summits of life it is a sacrament, and the most awful sacrament, perhaps, we can ever take, and the most certain, if we take it unworthily, to bring damnation. But from the rudest and most brutal savage, to the truest American, marriage,— the loftiest and best, as I believe, on the planet,— it is always, in some sense, the same thing that is done in this union. It turns the man and woman into husband and wife, creates the beginning of a home, insures a true and welcome identity between parents and offspring, binds life together between one generation and another, and out of the kingdom of Nature helps to bring the kingdom of God. "For marriage," Bishop Taylor says, "like the bee, builds a house, and gathers sweetness, labors, and unites into societies and republics, keeps order, exercises many virtues, promotes the general interest of mankind, and is that state of good to which God has designed the present constitution of the world."

Marriage is a divine institution, because there is a divine reason for it in our life. So, when Jesus said, "A man shall leave his father and mother, and shall cleave to his wife, and they twain shall be one. What God, therefore, hath joined together, let no man put asunder;" it was the sequel and conclusion to what he had said a moment before, that God had made it so in the beginning. A true marriage is, therefore, always a religious act in itself, because religion means the binding of one to another, whether it be on earth or in heaven, in a true and pure union. So the Scriptures never command this relation; they only recognize, and bless, and guard it. Everything seems to be settled once for all, from their own beautiful and holy vision of it, when the man wakes before the fall, sees the woman that God has brought to him, recognizes her as a part of his very self, takes her to his heart, and God is there as the witness, and blesses them.

Marriage, in the Bible, stands forth as a divine fact, rather than a divine commandment: it is intimately one with our creation. The blessing of God is already within that on which the minister calls the blessing of God to descend. To a true wedding of two human souls and lives nothing can be added but religious ceremonial and the proper social safeguards. The man and woman, in a true wedding, become husband and wife, because their Creator made them for each other, just as much as he made Adam and Eve for each other, and brought them face to face, as he did in Eden. And so when it is really true to those who take part in it, the good old-fashioned Quaker wedding is nearest the truth of God, in which the man and woman declare, as the ground of their union, that they have been moved to this deed by the Holy Spirit. That declaration not only brings the Lord to the marriage, but makes him also the match-maker; and it must be for this cause, in its measure, that so large a proportion of the Quaker matches turn out well. But every true match is made in heaven; and all true men and women who believe this, and act on it, find something of heaven in their match; so that John Brown of Haddington was not so far wrong when he felt the time had come for him to enter the holy estate, and that he had seen the woman the Lord had made to be his wife, and went to tell her so; and the good soul knew what he had come about, and was just as sure as he was that she was meant for him, and he for her. Yet he said, "My dear madam, you know what I am going to say; but, if you please, before I say it, we will ask a blessing." And that was what they did.

It is the experience of all times, and no doubt of all peoples, that men and women are made for each other, to be husband and wife, and are very often brought together by a providence they cannot account for, and they can never be separated in their souls any more. A young man goes into a room of an evening, with a heart as free as an unmated swallow, and comes out of it sixty minutes after a captive for life; and the maiden knows what the youth knows, and in her heart says amen to the revelation, though it may take her some time to say it with her lips. I have a friend, a man of great intelligence, who told me that when he was in the middle of the Pacific on a voyage, he saw a face in a dream, and it was borne in upon him that this was the face of his wife. He went through many adventures after that, was away about seven years, came back, went home, went to a quarterly Quaker meeting in Bucks County, Pennsylvania, and there saw in a Quaker bonnet, for the first time with his human eyes, the face he had seen in his dream. The maiden became his wife; and I never saw a happier pair on the earth, or a sweeter home or children; and I have no doubt of the perfect truth of the story. All true marriages are made in heaven.

> " All true love is blessed with reverence,
> As heavenly light is blessed with heavenly blue."

Any true observation of the life we are living will bring the assurance that marriages of this sort are by no means so few as cynics and satirists would like us to infer. If from thirty to forty years of intimate observation, in two widely separate sections of society, — two worlds, and the intimacy of a minister beside, — can be of service in forming an opinion, it is mine that a great preponderance of the men and women who become husbands and wives, find their helpmates, their matches, the one human being they need to make up the full measure, so far, of their life, in the man or woman they marry.

It is probable they may not find what I may call their ideal man or woman — the wonderful person the romances can make so much better than the Lord of life makes us, as the pictures in a fashion-plate are finer than the portraits of the masters. When we form our taste on this sort of standard, we are likely to be disappointed, and ought to be.

It is possible, too, for many reasons, that in the truest match which the Lord himself can make, there will be times when the husband and wife cannot see eye to eye, or make one music of the bass and alto in which they plighted their troth. It is extremely probable if a man cannot always feel satisfied with himself before he is married, he will not always feel satisfied with his wife after;

and if she sometimes charges herself with folly when she is a maiden, she may do the same now and then by her husband when she is a wife. If my self-love cannot hide or extenuate what is wrong in myself always, it must be a very tender, and holy, and everlasting love that will steadily overlook what may be wrong in another that I only love as well as myself. I know of nothing in the structure of this universe, or in life, or in the Bible, that can bear me out in the idea that a doubled possibility of happiness, in the addition of another life to mine, ought not to bring just that much more trial also: twice the felicity implies twice the infelicity in every other direction. The most exquisite organization is always exposed to the most appalling pain.

This possibility of falling out is in some way to be expected then; in what way, we cannot well foresee, and it is not best we should. It may be health, or temper, or habit — it is no matter; there must be trial of our faith in each other, as there is of our faith in God, and some doubt now and then of each other's love, as there is now and then of the diviner love of Heaven. No man or woman has any business to enter into this intimate oneness of life and soul without such an expectation. When the lark soars and sings over a mountain tarn, his shadow is as deep in the water as his soaring is high in heaven. Wise old Bishop Taylor says, " Marriage has in it less of beauty than a single life, but more of safety. It is more merry, but also more sad. It is fuller of joy, but also of sorrow. It lies under more burdens, but is supported by the strength of love, so that these burdens become delightful."

Something like that is to be expected in the very nature of things; it is to be found as the shadow cast by the truest and purest light that ever shines in a home. The sweetest wife that ever lived has said things to her husband scores of times that she would allow no other human being to say about him, or, once for all, that third person must hear a piece of her mind, if it were in a prayer meeting; and the truest husband will now and then make his will known to his wife in tones so imperious, that, if he heard another utter them to the same woman, it would bring him leaping, like a leopard, at the scoundrel who dared to speak so to the mother of his children.

"Jack," we said to our journeyman when he had been down home once, "Jack, what is the matter with thy head?" "Going past such a cottage," Jack said, sheepishly, "I heard the woman scream. I knew he was not over good to her, and I thought that was too bad. So I rushed in, and got hold of him, and was trying to get him down, and then the wife hit me."

It was an illustration, from a range of life among the Yorkshire hills, that was little better, thirty years ago, than savage, of a principle that holds good in the sweetest and best of the land, where the uttermost hurt is a sharp word that is repented of and forgiven the moment it is spoken. Husbands and wives, when they are wise, understand and act up to it, as the condition of being what they are, and bear and forbear within all fair lines and limits.

With these elements in marriages, and forming a part of their very structure, my observation convinces me that the true match is the rule. In the overwhelming majority of instances, those that came to be husband and wife were made to be husband and wife. Very often in the face of our sins and follies, by the tender mercy of God and not at all by our deserving, the great gift is given that makes a heaven for us where sometimes we would have made perdition for ourselves; and sometimes the blessed life comes of honor and truth, life-long, in those that are made one in it; but to believe that disappointment and misery come of the majority of marriages, is like believing that in this world the devil has dominion over most souls.

John and Mary sit in their home, and wonder how Thomas and Susan manage to make so brave a show of their small stock of esteem. Thomas and Susan shake their heads now and then about John and Mary. But you find that somehow within it all there is better with the worse, as there is worse with the better. Very tender and true are they all when sickness smites them; very sorely they weep together over little graves. And then, if they must part, and one goes to the long home and one stays in this, whatever they, who are left to mend the poor broken life, may do, is well done, if they do it modestly and truly, and it has the blessing of the Risen One upon it. But then, in that case, it is always one more in a heart made larger to hold one more, never one cast out to make way for another. The match made in heaven is never unmade.

It is quite true, however, that with all this, there is a great deal of trouble in this land of ours, not to speak just now of other lands, rising directly out of this relation of husband and wife — trouble that does not lie, or cannot be brought within the lines I have tried to draw, but breaks out and flames up before the world, draws the attention sometimes of a community, and sometimes of a nation, connects itself not seldom with some dreadful tragedy, and compels us to ask what we can be coming to, and whether there is not to be a complete disruption of the old social order, — liberty running into license, love driven from her throne by lust, and this new land of promise put to shame, and brought to ruin by the vileness that destroyed the old.

It is very clear that here is something for all of us to ponder who have children coming up, who must take their chance with this growing trouble; may be smitten by it as certainly as other people's children are smitten now, — God pity them; or whether we have children or not, for all of us who love their land, and nation, and God and his truth, and the commonwealth of the world. It is natural, and must be useful, I think, to try to find where the reason lies for these appalling evils, that do not merely threaten us, but are on us; and whether plain and well-meaning people can use these reasons, either for prevention or cure, or what cure there may be for this great trouble that seems to grow and spread as we are looking at it.

Is it not possible for a man and woman to make sure when they marry that they are to be true husband and wife at the cost of the usual pains and penalties that will always insist on their own payment, and ought never to be thought unreasonable? Is it not possible to make this natural and beautiful law of our life all but universal, that for the man there is a woman, and for the woman a man, who will be a true counterpart? and that they shall know it, or else know they can never marry, because, without that, the license and minister's blessing are the merest farce that was ever acted. I cannot but believe there is such a safeguard — a true light, that lighteth every man who will follow it — about this, as there is about truth, and honesty, and justice, and honor. I believe we can hardly make a mistake, except we insist on doing it, about this most essential thing in our whole career. When marriage brings misery, as a rule, it is not by providence, but by improvidence, and we suffer in that for our sin very often in something else.

And I would venture to name this, as the first reason why troubles come that can never be fairly met, and very worthy men and women get so badly mismated, — that the whole habit now of young people, as they see each other with any thought of ever being husband and wife, is the habit of semi-deception. They set themselves to deceive the very elect, by always putting on an appearance, when they are in each other's company, that is no more true to their nature, than the noble uncle is true they see on the stage, who flings his thousands about as if his banker's balance was a splendid joke (as it is), and then goes home and scrimps his wife and children of their barest needs.

In the more simple life of the country, where marriages are made that generally turn out well, the man and woman know each other intimately. They go to school together, and singing-school, and apple-bees, and huskings. The man knows the woman's butter, and bread, and pies, by much experience; and the woman the man's furrow, and swath, and seat on horseback; and as for temper, have they not fallen out and made up ever since they could run alone?

But in time we rise in life, and move from the farm to the city, exchange the kitchen for the drawing-room, linsey-woolsey for silk, and blue jean for broadcloth. The young gentleman comes in his Sunday best, and takes the young lady to the concert; walks home with her from church, and stays to tea; admires her touch on the piano, and her opinion of Mrs. Browning; and she, his superior air, and whatever beside may take her fancy, including, very often, his report of the money he makes, and can make; and that is really all they know of each other,— and that is less than nothing, and vanity. God forgive them! It is a game of cards, in which it is of the first importance to both not to reveal their hands; but the revelation is made at last, and they find that both intended to cheat, and did what they intended.

Of all the things needed now to make a true

and happy marriage, it seems to me that honesty, reality, and a sweet and simple intimacy, are the first. There is a conventional prudery about our young people, which must be as bad as it can be. If the young woman is making bread when the bell rings, and the servant says it is Mr. Cypher, there is a rush to the dressing-room to put on a silk and a simper; and Mr. Cypher probably smells of cloves. I tell you this is wicked, and false as hell. I wonder things are not worse than they are. Young men and women must come as near as possible, in all pure, innocent ways, to that intimacy with each other before they marry which they must come to after, or they have no right to expect good to come of their evil. "Young women make nets instead of cages," Dean Swift said. If he had not been an ingrain villain in his relation to women, he would have added, "and young men do that also." It is bad on both sides. One of the greatest evils leading to the greatest of all, is this total want of frankness and honesty each to the other, in those that must one day be one.

Great trouble comes again out of the mistake that always has been made, and I suppose will be for a long time to come, that the attraction that ends in wedlock is an outer rather than an inner fitness. A winning face and form, though there be nothing within, count for more, with great numbers, than the sweetest graces of the mind and soul. So one marries a doll and another a dolt, to find in a year or two that they have made a mistake life will not be long enough to repent in and get righted. There is no intimate and ultimate fitness in a man and woman to make them husband and wife except the fitness of mind and character. Beauty will always be an attraction, and it always should be: God has ordained it so. And somewhere in this world, for the beauty that is merely in form and feature, there is always somebody who will rejoice with joy unspeakable, and never repent; and great beauty not seldom goes with great goodness. But in this most solemn transaction to which two human beings can come, all these questions are swept aside, and wait for the question of fitness to be settled first. Are these two the counterparts, not of dark to blonde and the underline to the overline in stature, but of thought and feeling, of habit and tendency of life and soul? because, as a rule, these we cannot alter, any more than we can alter decimals. That is what the Lord means when he bids the man and woman seek each other for husband and wife.

Then again, I will venture to say, the truest wedded life can only come out of the truest unwedded life. It is blank folly to imagine that a woman who has had half a dozen affairs of the heart, as they are called, can wed a man who has sown his wild oats, and make a happy match of it. "Who shall ascend into the hill of the Lord? Who shall abide in his holy place? He that hath clean hands and a pure heart, who hath not lifted up his soul unto vanity, nor sworn deceitfully." You say, that means the merchant and the politician, and the man and woman who would experience religion in the purest and loftiest sense. I say it means a fitness for a true wedding, as certainly as any other thing we can think of. There is no reach in our life in which these great first things can be more essential, either for this world or the world to come. I will enter into no particulars: you know all these as well as I do. You can say it is seeing life;

I say it is seeing death: it is building a closet to hold a skeleton in the Holy of Holies.

Purity and truth, as absolute as that of the angels of God, each to the other, from the day you plight your troth to the day you die, are also imperative; not in deed alone, but in thought and word; and not only towards others, but in your own most intimate life. There is a fornication of the eyes, Jesus says; and leaves us then in no doubt about his meaning. He means, that men and women may see each other's beauty and grace with eyes full of reverent admiration, and that shall be a blessed sight to them; or they may look on the same sight with eyes full of lust, and then their hearts are set on fire of hell. There need be no more sin beside that evil glance; there is fornication from that moment in the substance of the soul. I touch no impossible mountain-peak of purity when I tell you this. I stand among sweet home places, where the best men and women live the truest wedded life to be found on this planet, and the only life the husband and wife can live worthily.

And then this one word more. The wife is

still placed by law and custom on the footstool, while the man is on the throne. It is all wrong; and the time is coming when they shall "sit side by side, full summed in all their powers." Until that day dawns on the world, we must keep its morning star shining through our own windows. That wife is the rare exception who does not bear a full half of the burden, and as good Mrs. Payser says in the story, "Earn one quarter of the income and save another." It is the simplest justice, when she does this, to give her, not one third, but one half of all that is left when we are through. The truest thing to do, if the husband dies first, is to leave everything to the wife, exactly as the wife, if she dies first, leaves everything to the husband. Every will should be drawn in that way, as the last expression of our mutual love and trust. I have read wills made in this city, by men who died in the odor of sanctity, over which I should think the devil would chuckle, so true they were to the constitution of his infernal kingdom.

A pure life, from the day we become responsible to the moment we are revealed to each other; a frank and open communion from that day to the wedding; loyalty, purity, and patience mingling with our love from that day onward, and this true expression of our perfect trust from beyond the grave, — these are the things that go to a true wedding, a true home, and a blessed home life.

XI.

CHILDREN AND CHILDHOOD.

LUKE ix. 47, 48: "Jesus took a child and set him by him, and said unto them, Whosoever shall receive this child in my name receiveth me; and whosoever shall receive me receiveth him that sent me."

IT is very good to me, in reading the Bible, to notice how much of the interest and hope of the world is made to depend on the children that are unborn when the hope springs up, resting far away in the future, but sure to come when God will, and to bring with them some great blessing and help. The world moves on through the ages, and the generations come and go, each bearing its own burden, and fulfilling its own destiny; and to every one there is allotted a certain share of disappointment and sorrow, and the failure of hopes and expectations. But like a strain of clear, quiet music running through a tumult of clashing discords, the promise of the children to be born, who shall do what the fathers failed to do, runs through the generations, from Adam to the advent of the Holy Child. And when at last this child is born, and has passed through his wonderful career, and dies on the cross, so strong is the conviction that it is in the birth of the babe, not the death of the martyr, that the deepest meaning is hidden, that the new era, the year of our Lord, as we call it, dates from the manger, and not from the cross ; and then, though the preponderant weight of the church seems constantly to have been cast into the balance for Easter, and though twenty books have been written and twenty sermons preached about Calvary to one about Bethlehem, they have never as yet disturbed this steady human instinct that has left Easter to the church, and taken Christmas into the home ; has replied with a carol to every sermon, and insisted that the greatest day of the two was that on whose morning the stars shone right on a stable, and the angels sang about "Peace on earth, and good will to men" because a babe was born, and was sleeping, as they sang, in that rude, dark place.

This, I say, is a remarkable quality in our Bible. It is no less so as a fact in this common life to which the Bible is a perpetual index and inspiration. What was true in that old world, is still true in the new. The hope of humanity, the promise of the world to come on this planet, rests in the children. When the Spartans replied to the king, who demanded fifty of their children as hostages, "We would prefer to give you a hundred of our most distinguished men," it was only an expression of the everlasting value of the child to any commonwealth and to every age. They had been defeated, but their hope was that the children would conquer. They had done their best, but their children, they hoped, would do better. Sparta would rise again from the cradle and the nursery. The new hands would do the new work, and the fresh hearts receive the fresh inspiration; and so, in the hope that still shone for Sparta, fifty children were of more value than a hundred fathers. It was a truth which every age has, in some way, to learn. The great hope is always in the new birth. It is in the next new life that God hides the next new thing the world needs for its use. The time comes when great discoveries stop short of their consummation for want of a new man, and no more new discoveries are made. When the church is certain to fail for the need of a new apostle to refresh the old truths or to announce the new; when the great movement that began with one reformer, will thin out like the circles on the water if it cannot be taken up and carried on by another, and when no new reform can find a man to storm us with great burning words and stand for it,— length of life and weight of wisdom can never do it. When a great man dies, and a nation weeps for his untimely end, if we had but faith like a grain of mustard-seed, we should grow glad again, through our tears for a timely beginning.

> "Mortals cry a man is dead;
> Angels sing a child is born."

The hope of mankind is not in the old life so much as in the new birth. If the Marquis of Worcester had lived even down to the days of Watt, nobody believes he would have added "Watt's steam engine" to his century of inventions. Franklin, at eighty-five, was as far, or farther than ever from inventing Morse's telegraph; Servetus and Priestley might have lived as long as Methuselah did, and they would never have done the work of Channing or Parker, of Wilberforce or Garrison, or Elizabeth Fry, or Lucretia Mott. "What shall we do?" the nation cries; "our great men are dying out." It is not in the hundred distinguished men, but in the fifty undistinguishable children, that our hope lies. This preacher has got almost to the end of his tether; but there is a three-year-old child standing on a stool preaching to a three-year-old audience, who will win the world to a sweeter and nobler gospel in that very pulpit. All posterity stands before us in the presence of the children now in their cradles, or in the deep mystery of Providence towards which the world is always looking; and every generation begins the history of the world anew.

Now this, if I can see into the thing at all, must be the deepest reason that can be given for the unspeakable loyalty and reverence for children that so constantly filled the heart and life of Christ. He would teach us in this way to reverence this promise that lies in them, as we reverence God, because within it is folded all that is most glorious and good in the future. It seems to me, as I watch how the heart of Jesus is drawn to children, and how his arms are drawn about them, that he is always saying to us, " It is not only for their innocence, for their faith and trust, and for the heaven I see in their eyes, I do this, but because I know that within them, as the germ within the seed, and the seed within the earth, lies the whole future harvest of blessing to mankind ; " and I think if he had been on earth to hear that Swedenborgian say one Sunday lately, that the New Church of God on earth began in 1757, he would have replied, My friend, that is now a very old church, the new church begins now. Into a stable or a palace, the eternal Providence, to which you trust so clearly, has sent a child who will tell the new truth and found the new church again to-day, because the new church is not that which will garner the bones of a dead prophet, but that which will faithfully work out the will of God, as it is announced in these very moments by the prophet of the new time. I never said of Moses, what I now say of this little one, " He that receiveth him in my name, receiveth me, and he that receiveth me, receiveth him that sent me," because the hope of the world rests not in the sepulchre, no matter what may be its beauty and splendor, but in the nursery, though it be a stable.

I have tried to open this doctrine to this light, because I want now to consider some things that belong to it, as the branch belongs to the bole and the flower to the root.

If it be true then that the hope of the world lies in the cradle, not only that our life may go on at all, but that it may constantly reach upward towards nobler and better things, in what relation do we, who are now responsible for this new life, stand to it? and, as it is intrusted to our care, how do we deal with it? If to receive a little child in the name of Christ is so awful and sacred a thing, that when I do so I receive in some wonderful way Christ and God together into my home and heart, what am I doing about it; how much do I believe of it? Is the child and its childhood a very common and common-place thing, so that I am subjecting it to my convenience first, and then to all my whims after? or is it so great a matter that, like Israel with the ark, only the most sacred hands can be laid on it, and things done for it as it rests within and encloses the light and the shadow of God? And in saying this, I must fail of the first shred of the faithfulness that ought to stand like a wall of fire about every pulpit and preacher, if I did not here call attention to the outcry that is raised on all sides of us about the danger that is now threatening this nation through the baleful decrease in these blessed gifts from God that are the hope and treasure of the world, and in whom the fairest hope of this nation ought to rest. I need not say what a difficulty I encounter in touching on this matter in any way; I cannot tell you how impossible I have found it to put my meaning into words. But it is my advantage that I speak as unto wise men and women, who need no words of mine beyond this hint. I speak for that, however, which ought to give any man courage who has to deal with these sacred things in our life, when I say, that wherever this sin may hide itself, and under whatever name it may hide, the reason for it is no better than is, I believe, usually given. Then there is a word to say about it which goes deeper than that of the physician, the political economist, or the patriot. It is, that in some awful sense we refuse to receive God into our hearts and homes when hearing this voice saying to us, "Whoso will receive one of these little ones in my name, receiveth me, and he that receiveth me, receiveth him that sent me;" we break down the footway by which the divine nature was trying to cross over to us, and then think that somehow we have circumvented Providence. Foolish and vain then, as foolishness and vanity is our belief in Trinity or Unity; we may have the name of God, but we have put God away. Worthless as chaff our profession of receiving God in Christ; he stretched out his hands then, but we would not hearken. Let us pray, "Thy kingdom come"—we have barred its coming to the best of our ability, and if it come now, it will be in spite of us. O, friends, bear with me, you that are spotless, and let me speak, for there may be guilt somewhere, that my word and God's word may startle. I tell you, when this unspeakable offence is done to Heaven, the worst possibility is not what we may have taken from the measure, but from the hope, and joy, and fulness of life. It is, that in some way, we cannot even imagine, we may have made the whole world poorer by what we have done. What loss to this world, if once such a sin had been hidden away in Stratford-upon-Avon, or in the poor clay biggin two miles from Ayr in Scotland, or in the hut eight miles from Newcastle in England, or in many another place shielded and shrouded then, as our homes are now, but since then lifted up among the shining points of the world! It may be that it needs be such offences will come, but woe unto that man by whom the offence cometh. I could wish no worse hell for my worst enemy, if I ever take to bad wishing, than that one should haunt him in eternity, who might have come and poured a mighty treasure into the commonwealth of the world, but for that sin that kept him out of it. But I leave this painful possibility for the great positive truth of what is folded in the child and his childhood, and what we are to do about it.

And this must be said first, that if we are wise and faithful to our trust that have them, there is in each child the making of a man or a woman who shall be a blessing and be blessed. Men and women who shall add their mite to the wealth of the world, if it be but to smite with the hammer, or to stand at the wash-tub, and open a way by their faithfulness over one talent for the trust of two or ten. It is not for us to make our children great, but we all can do a great deal towards making them good. The divine ordination that will give to one one talent, to another two, and to another ten, it is not ours to control; but the Holy Spirit that will make the future man or woman faithful over that which they have, will be sure to come in answer to the prayer which is first a longing, and then a wise and loving endeavor that it shall be so. Great influences, which we cannot understand, stretching over the whole span of human life, will make one man as great as a Mariposa pine and another as small as a dwarf pear; yet in its degree this shall be as good as that, while the sun will shine, and the rain fall, and the blessing of Heaven rest on both. A wise and witty writer has said, that it is about equal to being canonized to marry into some families; but Jesus said, "Whosoever shall receive one of these little ones in my name, receiveth me, and he that receiveth me, receiveth him that sent me;" and then saying not a word about which little one he meant, or what family it would come from, he left the sweet faith undisturbed in every mother's and father's heart, that their own little ones can bear with them this best blessing as surely as any others, anywhere. The possibility, however, is that the little one may become not only good but great; goodness of itself may be greatness, as it was in Washington and Lincoln; or there may be greatness without goodness, as the vast catalogue of mighty men who have been the scourge and curse of the race can testify. But greatness and goodness in men like Chalmers and Channing among the preachers of this century, and others in every walk of art, and literature, and life,— these combine greatness and goodness together, and then they reach the loftiest place on which a man can stand.

This, fathers and mothers, is the deeper possibility which gathers about the children that have come to you from God, and bring God when they come into your home and life. They may be not only good but great — great and good together. Yet this is the hidden mystery that only God himself can reveal, as he reveals himself in the children he gives us. That small hand, tireless in mischief, cutting and hammering at things until you are distracted, may be then and there feeling its way towards some achievement in the arts that shall lighten all the burdens of life, and give man forevermore a new advantage in his strife with nature. There may be a surgeon, or a singer, or a preacher, or a painter, or a man deep and wise in science, or in government, or in the comprehension of mind or matter; or a woman in this better time that is dawning for woman, whose path shall be as the sun, shining more and more unto the perfect day, — these may be among those little ones coming up about you in the home, or whom you are teaching in the school, till you are so weary at your task sometimes that you hardly know what to do. This is the clear certainty, that besides the regular rank and file, — the men who are always needed to work in the common day of the world, — there must be mighty men in the new generation, as there have been and are in this. Preachers that shall win the world to hear them; reformers who shall storm it; statesmen who shall be its great ministers, and poets who shall be its chief singers, — all the men and women who are needed to make the next age greater and better than this, — and it will take no small pattern in anything to do that; — these are all coming through your homes; they are in their cradles, or waiting on the holy law of God for their time to be born. And they will come quietly into the world, in cities and backwoods, in the mansion and the cabin, and in the cabin more than the mansion, for the first-born sons of God always seem to take to the stable and the manger. Then in some way they will at last begin to give hints of the greatness with which they come invested. None will know it except their mother; and she will not understand it, but like Mary, she will ponder over it, and hide these things in her heart; then the day will declare it, and these great ones will take their place among the immortal men and women of the earth. But whether they will be great and good together, or only good; able to win the world, or only able to cultivate a little patch of its soil and raise some chickens; if we will receive them in the name of Christ, we receive Christ in them and God also.

Now what is it to receive a child in the name of Christ? In answering this question, I want to affirm that it would need no answer, had there not been so many mistakes made about this simple, natural, and beautiful truth; if one man, and set of men and dogmas did not insist that every child is wholly defiled by sin; needs to be purified in the atoning blood; to experience a change of heart; and be as soon as possible subjected to the torture that is called by these teachers "getting religion." The first time a father, lost in this delusion, looks on his sleeping babe, there is this shadow on its face cast by the defilement he believes in. So to him to receive the little one in the name of Christ, is to subject it to all the troubles which come in the train of the father's black foreboding; it is to be continually told of its depravity, until, perhaps, at last it believes in it; to be made a bond slave of the Sabbath, and of long prayers and longer sermons; and then at last, either to break away in desperation or be born again, by which change in children, good as it is in men, I often observe they leave behind them everything that is most natural and beautiful in their childhood, and, in giving themselves to God, wrench themselves away from all that one thinks God would love to see in children, if we may judge what he loves by the way he guides and inspires nearly all the children he has sent into the world.

With another, to receive a child in the name of Christ, is to subject it to an endless round of outward appliances; of catechisms, confirmations, and prayers said at stated times and in a stated way, until the sweet, warm life takes the form of the mould into which it is so carefully cast, and loses the beautiful fashion it brought from heaven, in getting ready to go there; as if in some other country a man should train his children for a future life in this republic, in which a certain self-command and power to meet all emergencies man-fashion, are indispensable, should fit them for this life by training them to the drill and pipe-clay of Austria or Russia. Indeed, this doctrine of what it is to receive a child in the name of Christ, is, I think, almost endlessly mistaken; while the true way lies open before us all, and is so clear, that if we were not pre-occupied with these other ways, I do not see how we could possibly mistake it.

For, if you will remember for a moment that double name by which, or by one of which, Christ was always known while he lived in the world, — the Son of Man, as he called himself, and the Son of God, as others often called him, — you will see at once this one true way that instantly closes all other ways whatever. For to receive a child in the name of Christ, is just to receive it in both these names, as the Son of Man and the Son of God; and then, accepting this fact that there, as it lies in the cradle or runs through your house, is a being bearing in its life this human and divine nature together; that it is your child, and the child of God; treat it as it becomes you to treat a being holding such a glorious inheritance; believe in the treasure that has come to you in this earthen vessel, and value it as it deserves; then that will be to receive the child in the name of Christ. It is first to receive the child as you would have received Christ himself, if your home had been selected as the one into which he should be born, and you had known what grace and glory was folded in the sleeping babe, and then to receive it as your own life back again, — the life of God and your life together; this to open out to the sun and wind of this world, and that to reach upward towards the better world from which it has descended to bless you, — The Son of Man, and the Son of God both, and both together; earth and heaven hidden in that crib in your chamber.

And so we come directly to the sight of two clear principles in our conduct toward these little ones; one is, that we shall guide and govern with our best wisdom and love the son of man, the life that is of the earth, earthy, the first man, as Paul calls him; and the second is, that we shall guard and reverence, with a faith and trust as great as we ever put into our worship of God, the Son of God, the life that is from above. I remember Harriet Martineau tells how, when she had grown to be quite a girl, a little one was born into their home; and as she would look at it, and ponder, not knowing what was to come of it, she got a terror into her heart that the babe would never speak or walk, or do anything she could do; because, she said, How can it, seeing that it is so entirely helpless now? But she found, when the right time came, the feet found their footing, the tongue its speech, and everything came along in its own time; and then, instead of the babe, she had a brother who was able to take her part, and teach her things who had taught him.

I presume it is her brother James she describes. And so the babe becomes an illustration, when he came to manhood, of the hidden greatness and goodness I have spoken of, together. But what I mentioned this for, was the illustration it gives of a very common latent fear in the hearts, not of sisters so much, as of fathers and mothers, that the life that has come to them, and is their life over again, will not scramble, or grow, or wrestle into its own place as theirs has done. They have no adequate belief in the hidden man folded away within the small frail nature, and that this man will walk among men, and talk with them as a man, and so they spend the better part of their time in trying to order afresh what our wise mother Nature has ordered already. This is all a mistake, every time. Make sure that the child will walk upright; that it has fair play to grow into a man or a woman, with as good guidance and as little interference as possible. Have faith in the Son of Man in the child, and if you are aware that there has been sin and folly in your own life, guard this new life as well as you can from the consequences of that sin and folly, and then you may be sure that there is quite as good a hope for the little one as ever there was for you. Give it freedom and fresh air, and all the teaching it can stand, without exhausting life in getting knowledge, and then trust the rest to God, as your fathers did before you; and if I know anything of the way of life, there will be a better chance in this new world and new time than there has been for yourself.

The guardianship of the Son of God in your little one is, perhaps, a deeper and more sacred matter; but it is all summed up in a word. Do whatever a father and mother may do to reveal to the child, not his baseness, but his holiness; not that he must be depraved, but that it is impossible he shall not be good and noble. When Dr. Arnold went to Rugby, the school was in a frightful condition, and it was considered clever and manly to do the basest things, and then to deceive the master about them. Arnold never for one moment appeared to believe he was being cheated. He said, practically, "Boys, I will not believe in your depravity;" and then presently the boys were all saying, "What a shame it is to lie to Arnold, when he always believes you;" then the man's faith in them burnt up all the faithlessness in their hearts. Believe in the presence of God in the child, I say; and if you find you must do it, you may believe in the presence of the devil, too; but you must not, and cannot, believe in his masterhood.

When I was in New York once, I received a letter, together with a book, from a lady, a member of the Society of Friends. I found the book to be the Life of Isaac T. Hopper, I suppose one of the noblest men in his way this country has ever known, and in nothing more wonderful than in his perfect love, and trust in peace and good will as the true gospel of Christ. But the first chapter of the book is taken up with a recital of the deeds of mischief done by Isaac when he was a child. It is one of the most extraordinary chapters of childhood I ever read. The way that little fellow would astonish the good Quakers who came to see his folks, was a marvel. His pranks with pins and twine, and even gunpowder, cannot be told; not a doubt but many a friend went away feeling that if ever the unnamable incarnation of evil did get bodily into a boy, and stay there, that little Hopper was the "all possessed." But one thing was steadily there through all the wild pranks the lad would play, and that was, a certain quick reproof of conscience, — the good striving with the evil; and a wise mother was there to believe, as all wise mothers do, that what was good was very good, and the evil was never hopeless, and by God's good blessing on the boy, and her wise and loving care, it would all come right; and so she found, at last, they were more than conquerors. So the mischief of a child, who was only mischievous because he had more energy than he knew what to do with, became the strength of a man among the noblest and best of the good in this age. It is but one instance in a thousand of a nature so full of life in our own children, we do not know what we shall do with it; yet while we are fretting and foreboding, but still doing the best we can, the unslumbering Providence is, out of seeming evil, still educing good: touching the conscience when we do not know it; opening the new nature, in his own way to the new heavens and new earth; raising up a man to the Lord; when Jesus said, "Whosoever receiveth one of these little ones in my name, receiveth me, and he that receiveth me, receiveth him that sent me," he made no distinction as to the kind; they were all alike to him; they all held this awful and wonderful possibility for the future in their nature of greatness and goodness. So we must welcome little children when they come to us as the fresh presence of God in the world — the new creation on which, and in which, the whole future of the world rests in the love and grace of God.

XII.

TENDER, TRUSTY, AND TRUE.

Psalms xxxiv. 11-17: "Come, children, listen to me, and I will teach you how to serve the Lord. Never say bad words, nor what is not true. Go right away from what is bad; do good; try your best to be gentle and kind. Then the Lord will hear you when you cry to him in your trouble, and help you every time."

This sermon, as I said last Sunday, is all for the children, and not for the men and women: so I have tried to put the text into easy words, so that children may know what it means as soon as I read it. And I should like to make my sermon as plain as my text; then children will know what my sermon means too. Sermons are divided into three parts. I am not quite sure whether a sermon can be a sermon if it is not in three parts. At any rate, it is very useful to make three parts, for then you can guess how much more the preacher will say: and little Hattie Collyer told me one day, she was so glad when I said thirdly; for she knew then I should soon be done. Now, my three parts will be three all in one to-day; and every one will begin with the same letter. First, Tender; second, Trusty; and third, True: and I want in the sermon to say what will help you to be tender, trusty, and true. I am very glad that I have found such a nice good text to preach from; it is just what I wanted: and I hope you will take care not to forget the text. When I was a boy, I had a Bible I could carry to church in my pocket; then when the man said, "You will find my text in such a place," as I say to-day, I used to find the place, to put a mark in it, and then to read all about it when I went home. I wish this were done by the children in this school. I can tell you, children, it is a real good thing to do; for it will help you to know ever so much more than you do know about the best book that ever was printed, or it may be that ever will be printed, as long as the world stands. Well, now, if you read the text when you get home, and the psalm too, you will find that King David wanted to tell young folks what I want to tell you; that is, first, how to be good; and then what is the use of being good. And he does not say, "I think so," or, "It may be so," but, "It is so." As if he had said, "Now, children, you just trust me. I was once a child like you. I am now a man and a king. I can see away back to the time when I was a little boy, and begged honey from my mother, and cried when I didn't get it. I can tell just what was good for me, and what was bad; where I came out right, because I began right; and where I came out wrong, because I began wrong; and I want to tell you, so you may know what to do. Come, children, listen to me."

I can remember when I was in the Sunday school, and had just begun to read about David, that I did not feel sure he ever was a real baby, and had to be fed with a teaspoon; or that he ever was a real little boy that went to school as I did, and played marbles, and had to knuckle down, and had a peg-top, a jackknife, some slate pencils, ever so many buttons, and a piece of string, all in one pocket; that he ever had to try hard not to cry when he went to school very cold mornings; or that the teacher spoke sharp to him when the little chap had tried his best to get his lesson, and did not get it very well. But you know ministers have got to find out all about such men as David; and I have found out enough to make me feel sure he was once a little boy, just like one of you; and had to get verses, like you; and didn't like it, like you: that he did not like to go to bed early, like you; or to get up early, like you. I rather fear that, in the summer, he ate green apples, unripe melons, hard peaches, and sour plums, as you do; and got sick, and was very sorry, and had to take medicine, as you do; and said he would never do it again: and then I believe he never did do it again, after he promised not to; which I hope is like you also. Now, just here I was trying to see what sort of boy David was when he grew bigger; and, as I shut my eyes, and so tried to see it all clear, I heard a noise right under my study window. This was about four o'clock, Friday afternoon; the schools were out, and the children running home. I turned my head to see what was the matter, and then I saw what I want to tell you. About ten boys were standing together. All at once a big boy knocked a little boy down, and rolled him in the snow. The little boy got up, and said, "What did you do that for?" Then the big one drew off, as if he was going to do it again; and I believe he would have done it as bad as before, but the small boy walked sobbing away towards home.

"There," I said, when I had seen that, "I know what David never did do: he never struck a boy that was no match for him; he never was a coward like that; for he is a coward to strike a small boy so; and those others are not the boys they ought to be, to stand by and see it done." I saw such a thing in a picture once; it was called the Wolf and the Lamb. A great, cruel boy meets a small, delicate lad who has lost his father, and stands over him with his fist doubled, just as I saw that boy stand under my study window. I think if any boy in this church were to see that picture, he would instantly say, "What a shame to use a boy so who is not your match!" Once I read in the Life of Dr. Channing, who was one of the best men that ever lived (a great deal better than David, because he lived in a better time), what he once did when he was a boy, and saw a thing like that. Little Channing was one of the kindest and most tender-hearted boys I ever heard of. I will tell you a story to show you how kind he was, and tender, and true. One day he found in a bush a nest full of young birds just out of the shell. Children, did you ever see a nest full of birds just out of the shell — little tiny, downy things, with hardly more feathers than an oyster? These birds were just so when William Channing found them; and when he touched them with his finger, to feel how soft and warm they were, they all began to gape, very much as you do when I preach a very long sermon. Well, little Channing knew the birds did not gape because he preached a long sermon, but because they were hungry. So what did he do but run right away, get some nice soft crumbs, and feed them; and after that, every time school was out, he ran to feed his birds. But one day, when he went to the nest, there it lay on the ground, torn and bloody, and the little birds all dead; and the father-bird was crying on the wall, and the mother-bird was crying on a tree. Then little Channing tried to tell them that he did not kill their poor young brood; that he never could do such a mean, cruel thing as that; that he had tried to feed them, and help them along, so they might fly. But it was no use; he talked baby talk to them as you do to your little sister. They could not understand him, but just kept on crying; so then he sat down and cried too. Now this was the sort of boy Channing was; and I was going to tell you that one day he heard of a big boy beating a little one, like that one under my window. Channing was a little boy; he was a little man when he was full grown; but then he had a big soul. I was going to say he had a soul as big as a church; but indeed his soul was bigger than all the churches in the world;—and when he heard of that, he went right to the boy, ever so much larger than he was, and said, "Did you strike that little boy?" "Yes, I did; and what then?" "Then," said Channing, "you are a coward, because he was no match for you; and now I am going to whip you for doing it." Because he had a big soul, though he was a small boy, he went in, and did handsomely; and that was the only time he ever fought in his life. And I, standing in this pulpit, honor him more for it than if he had never fought at all. Boys, I like peace; I like to see you play like good, truehearted little men. Never fight if you can help it; but never strike a boy who is no match for you, and never stand by quietly while another boy is doing it. Tender and true, boys; tender and true. King David, King Alfred, George Washington, William Channing, Theodore Parker, more great men than I can name, were all that sort; and they came out right because they went in right. Brave as lions, true as steel, with kind hearts for doves and ravens and sparrows, they would never tear birds' nests, or sling stones trying to kill birds, because they felt as Jesus did when he said, "Blessed are the merciful."

To see David when he was a boy, you might think there was not much in him, because he was so tender-hearted; because he would not strike, or pinch, or prick with a pin, a boy that was no match for him, or take his jackknife, or split his top, or spoil his kite. But look out for a tender-hearted lad. I tell you, he can flash, and strike too, when the right time comes. Why, just look at this very David! One day, when he had grown big enough to stay with the sheep, there came along a bear, and another day a lion; and each of them seized a lamb, and was making off with it. Now, what do you think that boy under my window would have done if he had been in David's place? I believe he would have run away, and left his sheep. What did David do? I will tell you. He had a staff, you know, made out of good sound wood, with a crook at one end and a spike at the other, and both times he made after the wild beast; gave him, I suppose, the hardest knock he knew how to give with the crook, and then fought him with the pike. There was a soldier, living only six miles from our house when I was a boy, who fought a Bengal tiger once in India with nothing but a bayonet, and killed him after a tremendous struggle. I guess David had a hard time with the lion and the bear: but he says the Lord helped him; and I have no doubt he did. I believe the Lord helped little Channing to fight that big bad boy in Rhode Island, because Channing was on the Lord's side; and you know that the hymn we sing so often after sermon says, —

> "He always wins who sides with God;
> To him no chance is lost."

Which is just as true as gospel.

Well, then, there is another thing I want to say. These men I mentioned were not only good and kind, and true as steel, but, when they said a thing, you might be as sure it was true as if you had seen it twenty times over. I think David did sometimes get into mischief. I suppose he spilled the milk once; but I am sure, if he did, he did not blame the cat. I guess he tore his jacket rambling after olives; but if he did, I know he did not say a big boy tore it as he came home from school. I think he had to take a whipping now and then: if he had, I believe he just stood up, and took it like a man. This, children, this being true is a great thing. If you ask me which is worse, to be cruel to small boys and kittens and birds or to tell a lie, I really could not tell you. Now I think it is this, and then I think it is that: they are both as bad as bad can be. And now I want to tell you a little story of a little boy who was all three — tender and trusty and true; and then I will be through with my sermon.

Away off, I believe, in Edinburgh, two gentlemen were standing at the door of a hotel one very cold day, when a little boy, with a poor, thin, blue face, his feet bare, and red with the cold, and with nothing to cover him but a bundle of rags, came and said, "Please, sir, buy some matches?" "No: don't want any," the gentleman said. "But they are only a penny a box," the little fellow pleaded. "Yes; but you see we do not want a box," the gentleman said again. "Then I will gie ye twa boxes for a penny," the boy said at last. "And so, to get rid of him," the gentleman, who tells the story in an English paper, says, "I bought a box. But then I found I had no change: so I said, 'I will buy a box to-morrow.' 'O, do buy them the nicht, if you please,' the boy pleaded again. 'I will rin and get ye the change; for I am verra hungry.' So I gave him the shilling, and he started away; and I waited for him, but no boy came. Then I thought I had lost my shilling; but still there was that in the boy's face I trusted, and I did not like to think bad of him. Well, late in the evening, a servant came, and said a little boy wanted to see me. When he was brought in, I found it was a smaller brother of the boy that got my shilling, but, if possible, still more ragged and poor and thin. He stood a moment diving into his rags, as if he was seeking something; and then said, 'Are you the gentleman that bought the matches frae Sandie?' 'Yes.' 'Weel, then, here's fourpence oot o' yer shillin'. Sandie canna come: he's no weel. A cart run ower him, and knocked him doon, and he lost his bonnet, and his matches, and your sevenpence; and both his legs are broken; and he's no weel at a', and the doctor says he'll dee. And that's a' he can gie ye the noo,' putting fourpence down on the table; and then the poor child broke down into great sobs. So I fed the little man," the gentleman goes on to say, " and then I went with him to see Sandie. I found that the two little things lived with a wretched, drunken step-mother; their own father and mother were both dead. I found poor Sandie lying on a bundle of shavings: he knew me as soon as I came in, and said, 'I got the change, sir, and was coming back; and then the horse knocked me doon, and both my legs are brocken. And, O Reuby, little Reuby! I am sure I am dee'in! and who will take care o' ye, Reuby, when I am gane? What will ye do, Reuby?' Then I took the poor little sufferer's hand, and told him I would always take care of Reuby. He understood me, and had just strength to look at me as if he would thank me; then the light went out of his blue eyes; and, in a moment,

> 'He lay within the light of God,
>   Like a babe upon the breast;
> Where the wicked cease from troubling,
>   And the weary are at rest.'"

Come, children, listen to me, and I will teach you there is but one way: it is to be tender and trusty and true. Whenever you are tempted to tell what is not true, or to be hard on other little boys or girls, or to take what mother has said you must not take, I want you to remember little Sandie. This poor little man, lying on a bundle of shavings, dying and starving, was tender and trusty and true; and so God told the gentleman to take poor little friendless Reuby, and be a friend to him. And Sandie heard him say he would do it — just the last thing he ever did hear; and then, before I could tell you, the dark room, the bad step-mother, the bundle of shavings, the weary, broken little limbs, all faded away, and Sandie was among the angels. And I think the angels would take him, and hold him until one came with the sweetest, kindest face you ever saw: and that was Jesus who said, "Suffer the little child to come unto me;" and he took him in his arms, and blessed him. And then Sandie's own father and mother would come, and bear him away to their own home, for in our Father's house are many mansions; and there Sandie lives now. And I think that the angels, who have never known any pain, who never wore rags or sold matches, or were hungry or cold, came to look at Sandie in his new home, and wonder, and say one to another, "That is the little man who kept his word, and sent back fourpence, and was tender and trusty and true when he was hungry and faint, and both his legs were broken, and he lay a-dying." And Sandie would only find out what a grand good thing he had done when he was right home there in heaven. But I tell you to-day, little children, because, whether it be hard, or whether it be easy, I want you to be as tender and trusty and true as Sandie.

XIII.

PATIENCE.

James i. 4: "Let patience have her perfect work."

This apostle, in speaking of patience, intimates that it is not a belonging, but a being, a spirit separate, in some manner, from the human spirit, as the angels are; trying to do something for us, but only able as we will give it free course; so that his charge to his fellow Christians all the world over, to let patience have her perfect work, is not so much that we shall do something, as that we shall let something be done for us. All the help required of us towards patience, is not to hinder her working; then she will do all that is needed, in her own time and in her own way, and we shall be perfect and entire, lacking nothing. So that, when a man or woman says, "I will have patience," they speak closer to the truth than when they say, "I will be patient." To say, "I will be patient," has a touch of assumption in it; to say,

"I will have patience," denotes humility. The one word means, I will be what I will; the other, I will be what God will help me be. It is as if one man said, "I will be learned," and another said, "I will have learning." And a very brief reflection will enable us to see that the apostle is borne out in this happy distinction by the nature and grace of things as we see them all about us, and by what we feel within us. Patience is not there to begin with. It is no inborn grace, like love. It comes to us by and by, and tries to find room in our nature, and to stay and bless us, and so make us altogether its own.

The first thing we are aware of in any healthy and hearty child, is the total absence and destitution of this spirit of patience. No trace of it is to be discovered in the eager, hungry outcries, and the aimless, but headstrong, struggles against things as they are, and must be, but that never would be for another moment if these young lords and kings of impatience could have their way. But presently Patience comes, and rests on the mother's lifted finger as she shakes it at the tiny rebel, and puts a tone he has never heard before within the tender trills of her voice, and he looks up with a dim sort of wonder, as if he would say, What is that? But if the spirit be really and truly with the mother, it goes then to the child, and sheds upon him the dew of its blessing.

Then, in a few years, she looks at him out of the face of the old kitchen clock. It seems impossible that this steady-going machine should be so impassive, and persist in that resistless march; should not be quick to strike the hour he would drag before its time out of the strong heavens, or should not delay a little as he sits in the circle when the day is done, and dreads the exodus, at the stroke of eight, to his chamber. Poor little man! he has got into the old sorrow. It is not the clock, but the sun and stars he would alter, and the eternal ways.

Then, as the child passes into the boy, he has still to find this angel of patience. It is then very common for him to transfer his revolt from the sun to the seasons. If he is in the country, he rebels at the slow, steady growth of things; they never begin to come up to his demand. It is with all boys as it was with John Sterling. His father gave him a garden-bed, to till as he would; and he put in potatoes. They did not appear when he thought they should; so he dug them out, and put in something else; and so he kept on digging in and out, all one summer, because the things sprouted and bloomed at once in his hot little heart, like Jonah's gourd. It was an instance of the whole boy life. Nature can never come up to his notion of what she ought to do until Patience comes to help him. She shows him at last that the seasons must have their time, and he must bring his mind and action into accord with the everlasting order; for without that he can do nothing.

But every boy, of any quick, strong quality, struggles with things as they are and must be — wants to alter them to suit himself. It seems as if he had brought the instinct, but lost the memory, of a world and life that were just what he wanted; and he cannot give it up until this angel comes and helps him conform to his new condition, and he only minds her at last when he feels he must. The only children in whom she has her perfect work are those small martyrs that begin to suffer as soon as they begin to live, and are never released from their pain until God takes them to his breast in heaven.

There is no such patience besides as they show, as there is no such pity besides as they win.

But your big, healthy boy fights it out, hard and long; nothing is just as he wants it. Christmas comes like a cripple, and school, when the holidays are over, like a deer. It is a shame cherries and apples will not ripen sooner, and figures find their places more tractably, and geographies run as straight as a line. He knows no such felicity besides as to run to a fire, or after a ball, or to burn fireworks, or scamper away on a horse. The reason is just that which we always give as we watch him, when we say, "Now he is in his element." He is striking out, like a strong swimmer, on a splendid tide of impatience. He hears the mighty waters rolling evermore, and deep calleth unto deep in his heart.

It is easy to see, again, that these habits of the child and boy are only the germs of a larger impatience in the youth and the prime. We soon get our lesson from the angel about the kitchen clock, and the courses of the sun, and the limits of our power to make this world turn the other way. We learn to come to time, and set ourselves to its steady dictation in all common things; and patience, so far, has her perfect work.

I wonder to see the patience of some children, at last, about what they know they have got to do and be, in their tasks and strivings. I see small girls of ten who might well shame big men of forty as they buckle to their lessons, and go steadily through them; and even boys are sometimes almost admirable; though the angel of Patience must always feel about boys, I think, as that man in New York must feel, who keeps in the same cage the cat and the canary, and the mouse and the owl, with half a dozen more of the sharpest antagonisms of nature. Patience must feel about boys as that man feels about his animals, — that, after all his pains, there is no telling what they may do at any moment.

But if the boy does learn all he ought to learn about times and seasons, and tasks and treats, and lines and limits, it is very seldom that the lesson holds good as he begins the march to his manhood, or when he gets there. Patience, then, has to teach him deeper things: time still says one thing and his desire another, and he hungers again for what God has forbidden in the very condition of his life. But now it is unspeakably more serious than it was ten years ago, as she comes to him and tries to teach him her great lesson. She has to remember what myriads of young men, strong, and eager, and headstrong as he is, have broken away from her, after all, like the impatient prodigal in the Gospels, and have only come back and listened to her word when they had run through their whole possessions; and had to be patient under pain and loss, when they might have rejoiced with exceeding joy over powers incorruptible, undefiled, and of a perennial strength and grace.

Fortune and position, weight for weight, with what faculty the Maker has given him, is just as sure to come to a man in this country as the crop to the farmer and the web to the weaver, if he will only let this angel have her perfect work. The bee does not more surely lay up her honey, or the squirrel his nuts in store, enough to last until May brings the new bloom, and the tender shoots break forth in the woods, than a man, with the same temperate and enduring patience, can lay up life enough, and all life needs, to last him from the time when the frost seals his faculties to the new spring that waits where the Lord is the Sun. But what multitudes want to do, is to trust themselves to some short cut across the dominion of the sworn enemy of this angel.

Travellers in India tell us they have seen a magician make an orange tree spring, and bloom, and bear fruit, all in half an hour. That is the way many believe fortune ought to come. They cannot wait for its patient, steady, seasonable growth; that is all too slow, as the time-piece and garden-bed are to the child; they must put the time-piece forward, and that will bring thanksgiving, and gather their crop when they sow their seed. Patience comes and whispers, "It will never do; the perfect work is only that done by my spirit; the magician can never bring his thirty-minute oranges to market, because they can never nourish anybody as those do that come in the old divine fashion, by the patient sun and seasons." He gives no heed to the wise, sweet counsels; takes his own way; and then if he wins, finds that somehow he has lost in the winning; the possession is not half so good as the expectation: but the rule is, that the man who will not let Patience have her perfect work in building up his position and fortune, ends bare of both, and has nothing but a harvest of barren regrets.

No man, again, comes to middle age without finding that this is the truth about all the noble sensations that give such a color and grace to our life, and are such loyal ministrants to its blessing, if we can say "No" to the enemies of our good angel when they come and counsel us to disregard her ways, to let our passions take the bit in their teeth, and go tearing where they will.

Twenty years ago last June, when I had been a few weeks in this country, I tasted, for the first time in my life, an exquisite summer luxury; and it seemed so good that I thought I could never get enough of it. I got some more, and then some more, and then I found, for the first time, I think, what it is to have too much of a good thing. I ate, that day, of the tree of knowledge of good and evil; and now I care nothing for that good thing any more when I taste it. The angel is there with his flaming sword, insisting that I shall only eat of it out of Eden. It has been to me ever since a parable of this deep old verity. I disregarded the angel whispering, "You had better take care; if you eat that for a steady diet, through a whole June day, you do it in spite of me; the hunger for some more, which has been growing all your life, is a pledge that the good of this will abide with you as long as you live, if you will always let hunger wait on appetite." I had no idea of doing that. Impatience got the rein, and I gathered and ate the whole harvest of that good thing between dawn and dark. I mention this, because it is one of those experiences we all buy at a great price by the time we are forty, and then offer to give them away to young friends of twenty, but can seldom find anybody who wants them. In our youth, it is our misfortune, in a great many of these ways, to refuse to let Patience have her perfect work, and then to rue it as long as we live.

Every glass of wine, or dram of whiskey, drunk by a healthy and strong young man, is an insult and injury to this good angel, and makes it so far impossible for her to do her perfect work, because he is spending ahead of his income of life, and bringing a fine power of being to beggary, if not to worse than that. He can only get that glow and flame at a heavy discount, both of life itself and of all that makes life worth living. Patience would help him to infinitely finer pleasures from her simple and wholesome stores, and they would stay with him as long as he lived; but he will not listen to her counsels, and will have none of her reproofs; therefore will she weep at his calamities, and mock when his dole cometh.

This is but one way in which we can make this vast mistake through our impatience and desire to forestall the good that God will give us in his long, steady, seasonal fashion. There is a whole world of evils of very much the same sort, some more fatal still than the one I have named. It is the same thing whichever way we turn. Nature says one thing, and desire another. Only the perfect work of Patience can make both one, and then the result of both is grace. She comes to you, young men, as she came to us when we were young: some of you will put your life into her hands, as some of us did, whose hair is gray, and she will lead you forth into peace and joy. Some will refuse, and go for a short life and a merry one, and they will get the brevity but miss the mirth, and be dead at forty, though for twenty or thirty years after they may still remain unburied. Byron was a dead carcass long before he went out to the Greeks.

All this, in all these ways, as it comes to us from our infancy to our prime, is only the outward and visible part of a patience, or want of it, that touches the whole deeper life of the heart and soul, and makes the most awful or the most celestial difference to our whole being.

This is true, first, of our relation to one another. The very last thing most of us can learn of our relations to each other is to let Patience have her perfect work. Very few fathers and mothers learn the secret this angel is waiting to tell them about their children until perhaps the last is born. It is probable that he will give more trouble than any one of the others. If his own bent is not that way, the big margin he gets, when we are aware this is really the Benjamin, is likely to make that all right: we bear with him as we never bore with the first. Then love and duty were the motive powers; now it is love and patience. We would fain undo something now we have done to the elder ones, and the young rogue reaps all that advantage; and then the angel, by this time, has had her way, if Solomon, with his wicked axiom about sparing the rod and spoiling the child, has no more weight with us than he ought to have. She has shown us what power and grace are under the shadow of her wings, and how in each of these little ones we have another life to deal with, that is only fairly to be brought out to its brave, strong beauty, as the season brings out the apples and corn. Patience is the only angel that can work with love. To refuse her blessing is to refuse God's holiest gift, after what he has given us in the child's own being. I think the day is yet to dawn when fathers and mothers will feel that they would rather scourge themselves as the old anchorites did, than scourge their little ones; and will not doubt that they, and not the child, deserve it, when they feel like doing it. I suppose there is not an instance to be found of a family of children coming up under an unflinching and unfailing patience and love turning out badly; the angel prevailing with us prevails with the child for us, and turns our grace to its goodness. The fruit ripens at last all right, if we have the grace to let the sun shine on it, and to guard it from the destroyer. All the tendencies of our time to give children the right to have a great deal of their own way, are good tendencies, if we will understand that their own way is of course the right way, as certainly as a climbing vine follows the turn of the sun: all we have to do is carefully and patiently to open the right way for them wherever they turn.

Patience, again, must have her perfect work in our whole relation to our fellow-men. It is very sad to read of the shameful things that have been done in the name of Religion, for the sake of conformity: how the fagot has burned, and the rack has wrung. We cannot believe that we could ever do that, and very likely we never should; yet we are, most of us, inquisitors in our way, and want to force human beings into conformity with the idea we have of fitness, though it may not be theirs at all.

It is reported that the flitch of bacon at Dunmore, in Essex, is hardly ever claimed. It is a noble piece of meat, you know, always ready, with ribbons for decorations, and no little rustic honor besides, for the man and woman that have been married a year, and can say, solemnly, that their life, the whole twelvemonth, has been a perfect accord. Only once in many years is it claimed, though to many an Essex peasant it must look very tempting. The loss lies in the fact that they did not take this angel with them, and make her the equal of love. They imagine that love is omnipotent, and can guard them from that sharp word. Love very often leads them on to it, since love, they know, is justified of love; but when all hope of the flitch is lost, if they are true and good, the angel comes, and stays, and has her way. If they are neither, it is brute and victim, with no hope of even the questionable mercy that comes here through the divorce court.

Want of patience, indeed, apart from the vilest reasons, must be the main cause for the dreadful rank growth of this evil weed of divorce in our social life. There are, no doubt, instances in which to be divorced is the most sacred thing men and women can do. Many a woman must do this to save her life. She is tied to a beast that will crush her to death, and that is her escape. And many a man must do it to save his soul. It was a woman he thought he was wedding: he finds the old Greek fable, of something with a fair woman's face, but not a woman, was true; and she would drag him down to her den, if he could not get free.

But these are, on both sides, the rather rare exceptions. Trace the most of these sad things to the well-head, and it is want of patience, each with the other, that has made all the mischief, and what each will call, in their blind fury, an infernal temper, is this devil of impatience, which has taken the place of the good angel who would have saved them if they had welcomed her as they ought, and let her have her way. If they did love each other once, they will never find such blessing as could come to them, with patience as the aid to their affections. Human souls have an imperial quality in them; a turn for insisting on being master; and when they come so close together as husband and wife, and love recovers his sight, as he will, Patience must take up her part, and adjust the thing by a constitution of equal rights, and by an equal giving up of rights, or, in spite of love, there will come infinite trouble.

We have very much the same thing to learn in our relation to each other in the whole length and breadth of our life. Ministers with their people, and people with their ministers; employers with their servants, and servants with their employers; men in their dealings with men, and women in their judgments of women. We would all be very much more careful in what we say and do, if, when we pray, we should say, "Our Father, give us grace to let thine angel have her perfect work, to guide and keep us till we reach the line at which forbearance ceases to be a virtue; and then, if the storm must come, make it like the lightning that cuts its quick way through the clogged and dead atmosphere, only to restore and bless, to set all birds singing a new song, and deck the world with a new beauty,"—that would be a blessed prayer.

For, finally, there must be a divine impatience, too. Jesus Christ felt it now and then; but you have to notice that it is never with weakness or incompleteness, or even folly or sin; for all these he had only forbearance and forgiveness, and pity and sympathy. What roused him, and made his heart throb, and his face glow, and his voice quiver with a divine indignation, was the hollow pretence and ugly hypocrisy he had to encounter, and the judgments one man made of another out of his from a sense of superior attainment. That is our right, as much as it was his right, as we grow towards his great estate. I have seen an impatience as divine as ever patience can be; but this is needed only now and then, and can only come safely and truly to the soul in which her great sister has her perfect work. The perfectly patient man is always justified in all his outbreaks. Nobody blames the flaming sword, or the quick stroke home that comes from a noble forbearance, any more than we blame the thunderbolts of the Lord.

Last of all, for this angel of Patience we must cry to Heaven. One of the old pagan kings would not let the sage go, who came and told him that when passion was like to be his master, he would do well, before he gave way, to recite to himself all the letters of the alphabet. The counsel seemed so admirable, that the king cried, "I cannot do without you." It was only a dim pagan shadow of the sheen of the patient angel as the apostle sees her. There she sits, the bright, good servant of the Most High, ready to help all who cry to him. The good servant that, through untold ages, wrought at this world to make it ready for our advent; laying together, an atom at a time, this wonderful and beautiful dwelling-place, with all these stores of blessing in mine and meadow, mountain and vale; then when her great charge came, she was waiting for him, to nurse and tend him, own sister of faith, and hope, and love, and twin-sister of mercy; tireless, true, and self-forgetful, anxious only for her charge, and never to leave us, if we will let her have her perfect work, until, through all hinderance, she leads us through the golden gate, over which is written, "Here is the patience of the saints; here are they that keep the commandments of God, and the faith of Jesus;" then she will have her perfect work, and we shall be perfect and entire, lacking nothing.

XIV.

TWO MITES.

MARK xii. 43, 44: "Jesus said, This poor widow hath cast more in, than all they which have cast into the treasury: for all they did cast in of their abundance; but she of her want."

IN speaking to you briefly about this little personal history, I want you to notice, first, the difference between what this widow must have thought of her gift, and what the world thinks of it after almost two thousand years have come and gone. You can see, as you read the passage, that the words of Christ were not meant for her, but for those about him. He speaks after she has gone. It is very probable that she never heard of it as long as she lived, and not improbable that if she had heard of it, she would have minded it no more than any good and regular church-member now would mind what was said by one whom she considered heretical, dangerous, and not to be believed in. So she cannot have had the faintest suspicion that her gift would be remembered five minutes after it was given, or, if anybody noticed it, that they could possibly look at it as any more than the very poor gift of a very poor woman; and yet here it is, in its bare poverty, outshining the most generous giving the world has ever known. There is nothing like it, that I know of, in the Bible or out of it. A divine word has made gift and giver immortal. There she stands, with her half cent, in the sunlight of heaven, as the generations come and go, incorruptible, undefiled, and never to fade away. Those disciples who were to give us the Gospels, caught the words as they were said: " I say unto you, this poor widow hath cast in more than they all; for all they did cast in of their abundance, but she, out of her want, did cast in all her life;" and they could never forget them if they tried: then, when the Gospels had to be written, this must go in. It could no more be left out, than the great historic ruby can be left out of the English crown. Then the Gospels began to be read in distant places: Greece got them, and Rome, and Egypt, and Spain, Britain, and France, and Germany, and wherever they went the woman went, standing in the splendor of the divine words, so millions at last saw, what was seen at first by two or three, and still the glory grew: your fathers and mine, so long as we can trace them, saw what we see; and when we are dead and gone, our children will still see the widow standing with her two mites casting them into the store of the Lord, and then going back to her home, and beginning again, perhaps, to save two mites more. We turn over the same great book, and read how David and Solomon gathered their treasures, and gave them with generous hands for noble purposes; and how the people brought their gifts, when their hearts were stirred, and gave them freely for their temples and shrines, for worship, and patriotism, and charity; but we see nothing like this, — nothing that so touches the heart. "She, out of her want, did cast in of her life," and eternal life has come to her here on the earth; her giving has been her saving, and that half cent has brought millions of money to noble uses.

Again, we must not fail to notice that this divine word leaves us in no sort of doubt as to the reason why the poor gift should be what it was, in comparison with those which were intrinsically so much greater. Men seemed to give then, as they still give, with a vast generosity for good objects; and this treasury had two great purposes — the care of the temple, and the relief of the poor; both good, and both well cared for by the good men and women of that day; and Jesus saw what they gave; he was watching them. It is possible that he had been very much interested that day in the whole matter; may have gone again and again to watch, wonderfully moved and attracted by this sight of the givers and their gifts; and I think that I can see what he saw when he stood there that day, and can follow his thought a little way as I follow his eyes: the people pass the chest, each is dropping what answers to each nature, and then passing out of sight and out of mind, all except this widow.

Here comes a merchant; the times are hard, he tells you; nothing doing, taxes heavy, losses large, and things so bad generally, that you have to say, What a misfortune it must be to be a merchant! But you have to notice that his chariot is of the latest style, and by the best maker; his robes of the finest texture and color; his diamonds of the purest water; and, altogether, for a man in such hard trial, he looks very well. Yesterday, he looked over his accounts; he will not tell you what he saw there, but, certainly, he did not seem any worse for the sight. This morning, before he goes to his store, he will go to the temple; he will be thankful, to the extent of offering a lamb; and then there is a little balance, when all is done, that he would like to drop into the treasury. A little balance! but it would buy all that widow has in this world, — the hut she lives in, all the furniture, and all the garments she has to keep her from the cold. Very low the priest, who stands by the chest that day, bows to the generous gift; the holy man would be horrified if you told him he was worshipping a golden idol, but it is true for all that. Then the great merchant passes on, and you see him no more; he has given out of his abundance; he will not need to deny himself one good thing for what he has given. If a new picture strikes his fancy, he will ask the price, and then say, "Send that round to my house;" he will have his venison all the same, whether it is a sixpence a pound or a dollar; and at the end of the year he will have his balance undamaged, in spite of the hard times. He has given out of his abundance; but, considering the abundance, he has not given as the widow did.

Then there comes a lady. You can see that she is not looking well, and the world goes hard. This has been a hard year for her. She has had to give parties, and attend parties; to dress, and dance, and smile when she wanted to weep; and lose her rest, and be a slave that the slaves themselves, if they had any sense of what she is, and has to do, might pity. The season is over, and now she must think of her soul, — her poor soul. She must repent in dust and ashes; go to the temple; give to the poor, and to the support of the true faith; and, altogether, lead a new life. It is the most exquisite "make up" of dust and ashes on the avenue that morning. She sweeps on in her humility, gathering her garments of penitence about her, lest even a fringe should touch the beggar at the gate. She stops a moment to give her gift; low bows the priest again as she passes, and she takes her place among the women, and says her prayers, and her soul is shriven. May we venture to watch her back to her home, and see the luxury that waits her? Is there one jewel, or one robe the less for what she has given? or one whim the less gratified, when the time for penitence is over, and the season opens? I see no sign of that. I never hear her say, "This and that I will forego, that I may give." She has given of her abundance; she simply purchased a new luxury, and got it cheap, and she fades out of sight and out of life.

You see others come with better gifts, not so much, it may be, in mere money value, but more in those pure eyes that are watching that day, not for the amount of the gifts, but for their meaning. A decent farmer follows the fine lady, forehanded, and full of industry. His crops have done well; his barns are full; his heart is open. He has come to the city to sell his produce; has sold it well, and is thankful, and he will make his offering of two doves in the temple, and give something for the sacred cause, and to the poor besides, because his heart is warm and grateful, and, as he says, he will never feel what he gives to God and the poor; there will be plenty left at the farm when this is given; and then who knows but that the Lord will give a greater blessing next year, for does not the wise book say, "He that giveth to the poor lendeth to the Lord, and that which he giveth shall be rendered to him again"? So it is at once a free gift, and in some way, a safe investment. He is glad to give the money, and yet to feel that this is not the last of it. Very pleasantly the holy man smiles on him too, as he drops his shekels and passes on; he has been there before; he will come again. He is one of those fast friends who can always be counted on to give while the fruitful fields answer to the diligent hand. He is a sort of country connection to these commissioners of the Most High, and will always be received, as he is today, with grace and favor.

And very low indeed the good man bows to that stately centurion who comes now. He is not a member of this church; indeed, he is not a member of any church; for, like all his nation of that rank, he thinks that all churches are very much alike, and none of them of much account, except as managers of the common people. But it is a good thing to keep in with them; there is no knowing what you may want; and so he comes now and then, and looks on at the service, tosses his Roman gold into the chest, nods and smiles to the cringing priest, and feels that he has done well.

Then with all these come the good and sincere men and women, with not much to spare, but who make a conscience of giving, and manage to get an education for their children, and everything decent; who never want any simple and wholesome thing they need, and are able to lay up a little beside for a rainy day; as various as they are now, they were then, who would do something for these things which to them were so sacred; and it was when givers like these came, that the widow came with her two mites —the smallest matter, possibly, that anybody ever thought of giving. I think if she was like most women, the utter littleness of what she had to spare, would be a shame to her; she would be tempted, on the mere ground of her womanly pride, to say, "Since I cannot give more, I will not give anything: to put in these two mites when others are pouring in their gold and silver, will only show how poor I am." So it was like giving her life to give so little; and yet these two mites that meant so little to the treasury, meant a great deal to her. They meant darkness, instead of a candle on a winter's evening; a pint of milk, or a fagot of sticks, or a morsel of honey, or a bit of butter, or a bunch of grapes, or a pound of bread. They meant something to be spared out of the substance and essence of her simple and spare living. And this these wise and loving eyes saw at a glance. Jesus knew that the two mites were all she had; and so as they made their timid tinkle in the coffer, they outweighed all the gold. He saw what they came to, because he saw what they cost, and so his heart went with the two mites; and while the holy man, who had made such deep obeisance for the larger gifts, let this trifle pass unnoticed, Christ caught up the deed and the doer, and clad them both in the shining robes of immortal glory.

And this incident naturally suggests, first,

that there may be more splendor in some obscure thing we never stop to notice, and would not care for if we did, than there is in the things that dazzle our sight and captivate our hearts.

We have all had to notice this among children. In homes where there are plenty of children, there is almost sure to be one who will do things that cost the life, run all the errands, make all the sacrifices, and bear all the real sorrows, but beyond that be a little nobody; plain, probably, and small, not brilliant, never appearing to any advantage — if she is of that sex, as very generally happens — beside her more brilliant sisters; "a good little thing," the whole family says, and takes all the rest as a matter of course, expecting the service and sacrifice as something that comes in the course of nature. This is the two-mite child of the family; the small piece of home heroism, of a worth surpassing all the gifts and graces of the household besides; the little one that Christ would see if he came and sat down in the house, and would call his own; and while we would want to see him notice those we are perhaps proud of for their beauty or brightness, he would say, "Suffer this little one to come unto me, and forbid her not, for of such is the kingdom of heaven,—she gives more than they all."

We notice this again in the church. Some naturally attract and win applause by their gifts. The eyes of the church are on them; their Christian life is a sort of ovation, a triumphal procession, and their ten talents tell wonderfully as they ring down into the treasury of the temple. Others, again, attract no more attention than this widow with her two mites. There is very little that they can do, and yet they do that little at a cost the rest can hardly imagine. They say their poor word, feeling all the while it is so very poor that it cannot make much matter, but they must say it, for that is their duty. They do their bit of work, and a very poor piece it is, as everybody can see; but it is the best they can do, and it has come out of their life. It is their sorrow that they cannot do more, but it is the joy of heaven they do so much, and they, and not the brilliant and talented, are the true great givers; it is the unseen and unnoticed heroism of Christian men and women that feeds the fires of goodness, and wins the well-done of the Lord. Those who have great gifts and graces, and offer them generously for sacred uses, are honored and blessed, if what they do is done with sweet sincerity. But it is those who have but a small gift, and give that at a cost the gifted cannot measure, whom the eyes of Christ rest upon with the tenderest light, and of whom he says, "These give more than ye all."

And this that is true of the home and the church, is true of the whole life we are living. There are men who will some day win good places in the world, attract attention to what they do, win applause and honor for their deeds, but who may really be doing better now, when nobody knows or notices, than they will do then, because what they are doing now demands more self-sacrifice than they will ever think of in their greater estate. And there are tens of thousands in this nation, whom we never heard of, and never shall, whose deeds, weighed in these divine balances that weighed the widow's two mites, prove them to be more heroic in the heart and soul of heroism than the vast majority of those we have sung about and wept over,— the brilliant and attractive characters who gave out of their abundance, when these did cast in their life.

Then, again, we cannot be in any doubt as to what lies at the heart of this word of Christ, or what led him to cast that glory on a poor, desolate woman, and give her precedence over not merely the pomp and vanity, but the real grace and generosity of those who came with her. It was an illustration to him, and he will make it one to us, of this law of our life, that the most Godlike deed is that which belongs to the sacrifices we make, giving for sacred things and causes that which costs us most, and is most indispensable, and yet is given back to God. Nothing was worth a thought in this poor thing's gift but the sacrifice it cost her to give. Her two mites were as worthless, for any outside uses, as the smallest coin we can muster now would be in this church and in the Citizen's Relief Society. The whole worth of it lay in that piece of her very life which went with it; but that made the two mites instantly outweigh the whole sum of silver and gold cast in by the wealthy, which cost nothing, beyond the effort to give what a very natural instinct would prompt them to keep. They gave of their fulness, she of her emptiness; they of their strength, she of her weakness; they of their plethora, she of her hunger; they of the ever-springing fountain, she the last drop in her cup. It was not the sum, but the sacrifice that made the deed sublime, and set the doer, in her rusty old weeds, among the glorious saints and angels.

Surely this must tell us what it did to these that stood by the Messiah. The principle now is exactly the same as it was then, as certainly as any principle governing matter in natural laws. The young man may say, "I am willing to do my share for sacred causes and institutions;" but if he means by that, he will aid them after he gets all his parties, and operas, and sleigh-rides, and everything besides that his heart can wish, — the gift for which he will not deny himself the least of these things, must be before Heaven less than the least. And the man of business may say, "I will help; the Lord has been good to me, I will be grateful;" if gratitude takes the form of that he can well spare, and yet spare nothing out of his life. But after he has purchased with the talents God gave him as a steward everything for himself that he can possibly need, then he really spares nothing, makes no sacrifice, gives only out of his abundance, and is still open to that touch of fear, that he may not even be dealing fairly with the Principal who has committed the talents to his trust; the fear, which good old brother Cecil used to say, always gathers about stewards and agents that grow uncommonly rich. So may we all give, no matter what we are, a poor selvage out of the web in our ample and voluminous robes; give the crusts after we have eaten the dinner; spare in the Lent what we could not spend in the Carnival, — and it will be the same to every one of us. The wise all-seeing Eyes will see us, and what we are doing, and the angel will write in his book of life, " He gave to God and good uses what he did not need himself for any uses." Or we may give out of the real substance; but if we do not give with a real sacrifice, I have no authority from the Lord to say that the poorest Irish washerwoman in this town who gives to the Lord, according to her light, her two mites, which make one farthing, gives it out of her life to say a mass, even for the soul of her wretched sot of a husband who was found dead in the Bridewell, — does not take infinite precedence of the best and most generous who have all they want, and then do ever so nobly out of the rest.

For, once more, it is in its own way a piece of the grossest infidelity to presume that this incident at the old temple gates, that still stands out radiant in the light of heaven, was a chance observation, which might just as soon have been missed as not, and there had been no such lesson. Believe me, this cannot be true. The conjunction of the great stars is not more inevitable in the heavens than was this gathering to that sight and hearing on Zion. It was no chance that might or might not be; it was in the divine order, that we might be left in no doubt about this touching and deep-reaching truth. For so God will have us learn through his Son and an old widow woman who was moved in her poor soul to go out that day with her two mites, this holy and awful law of sacrifice, as it reaches into such things as these, — these common duties of being on the side of God in what we spare for the things that build up his cause or aid his children.

It was another lesson, indeed, that we learn, in this simple and most obvious way, of that whole world of grace and truth that culminates on Calvary. It is sacrifice in its uttermost simplicity, in words, as it were, of one syllable, fitted for babes in Christ. No more may we presume that there is not the divine observation of the human action on this lake shore that there was on that mountain top. The human eyes of Christ, as they looked with such tenderness on that sight, these human eyes were but the organisms through which God was watching, and the judgment pronounced when the deeds were done was from the judgment-seat of the Most High. So it is forever and ever. The divine eyes are watching us, with or without the human organism, and the words are said about us all sorrowfully when we are selfish and small, sweetly when we are self-forgetful and self-sacrificing. You may make a sacrifice, and feel very sad you could not do more; and go home when it is made, feeling that the thing is not worth a thought, and be glad to forget it yourselves, and only to remember the great gifts of the rich and generous, yet shall the last be first, and the least greatest. You shall say, Lord, when did I give two mites which make one farthing? and he shall say, You gave it at such a time, and went without such a piece of your life, that you might be able; and these shall say, That was when I gave my shekels; now will the Lord surely say, here is a crown of glory, and they shall cry out, "See what I gave, what I did at that very time;" and he shall say, It is not here; the angel has not made any record of it; it must have been out of your abundance; and we never reckon here the cup that was filled out of the ocean.

And if you say, we know all this already, and you have told us very much the same things before, I must still put you back, dear friends, on your own inner sense of what is right, and remind you of Paul's great word: "If thine heart condemn thee, God is greater than thine heart, and knoweth all things." If your heart has nothing to say about your duty to do more and to be more, and you know it is alive to the work God gives us all to do, then I am dumb. I want you only to put yourselves in the line of this holy and beautiful thing, this gem in the setting of the Gospels, to be sure that your gift to God is the gift of a part of yourself in everything you are called to give.

XV.

OLD AGE.

PHIL. 9 : " Such an one as Paul the aged."

OLD age is the repose of life,— the rest that precedes the rest that remains. It is the Seventh day, which is the Sabbath of a whole lifetime, when the tired worker is bidden to lay aside the heavy weight of his care about this world,— to wash himself of its dust and grime, and walk about with as free a heart as a forehanded farmer carries into his fields of a Sunday afternoon, at the end of harvest. For " old age should be peaceful," Dr. Arnold says, "as childhood is playful; hard work at either extreme of life is out of place. You must labor in the hot sun of noon, but the evening should be quiet and cool. It is the holy place of life, the chapel of ease for all men's weary labors."

But it has been the misfortune of old age to be generally unwelcome, with some noble exceptions among those who can see how nature never makes a mistake about time. The aged would rather be younger, and the young admire most in the old what they call their youthfulness; so that, "How young he seems!" is our finest praise of an old man, and "How old I feel!" is very often the old man's most pitiful complaint.

Now and then we come across a beautiful and contented old age, in which those who possess it seem to be aware how good that blessing is which can only come through a long lifetime, and give what their age has brought them. Such persons surprise us that we should ever have been content to admire in any old man or woman merely their poor traces of youth, while what is so much better than youth makes up the substance of every well-ripened life. It is as if one would persist in admiring the shrivelled petals that linger at the end of an apple, because they retain about them the dim memory of a blossom, and care nothing for the fruit that has come through their withering.

I am not to deny that we can find reason enough if we want it for this idea. There is plenty of evidence, to those that care to hunt for it, on the misfortune of growing old, from that outcry of the heathen, "Those the gods love die young," to the moan of the last man we found weary of his life, but loath to leave it. We can see sometimes in those who are growing old all about us such an isolation, passing at last into desolation, and such utter inability to bear up against the burden of the years, that we pray in our hearts we may be saved from an old age like that. Then we remember how Solomon called these the evil days, when we shall say we have no pleasure in them; and how a great philosopher wrote in the diary of his old age, "Very miserable;" and we can see Milton, sitting in the sun alone, old, blind, stern, and poor; and Wordsworth, walking in his old age by Rydal-water, but no longer conscious of the glory and joy of which he had sung in his prime; and a host besides, to whom old age has brought, as Johnson said, only decrepitude; and then we say with Lamb, "I do not want to be weaned by age, and drop like mellow fruit into the grave." We shrink back at our whitening hairs, and wonder how anybody could ever be so lost to the fitness of things as to call us — except in a sort of splendid jest — the old lady, or the old gentleman. The child longs for and welcomes his boyhood, and the boy the youth, and the youth his manhood. But very few and far between are the men and women who will desire their age, as a servant earnestly desires his shadow, or feel that the white head is a crown of glory, when they see in their own many threads of silver, and cannot hold it up for the burden of the years. In the face of this unbelief in the goodness and blessing of old age, I want to say, that no period of life can be more desirable than this, if it be what every old age ought to be; that old age is the best of all the ages, when it is a good old age, and it ought to be so considered. Such a conviction, as you may well believe who are still young, or in middle life, can only come fairly through a true personal experience; but this comes of itself: that if life be good as bud and blossom, and in its greenness, and the days when it is ripening, then there is no reason, in the nature of things, why it should not be good when it is fully ripe and waiting to be gathered. If the soil be good, and the sowing, and the seasons, then it is not a thing to mourn about that there should be a harvest. If the preparation and opportunity be good, what is to be said of the consummation? Can that be a thing to lament about, to beat back, a condition so unwelcome that it is polite not to be aware of its presence? I cannot believe in such a termination of these great, sacred processes of life. If it be a misfortune to grow old, it is a misfortune to be born, and to be a child, and youth, and young man, and in our prime. If the rest of our life is meant to be enjoyed, then this must have some better meaning in it than to be endured. It must go up and stand with the rest, or they must come down. Old age is a beautiful consummation, or it is a bitter mistake.

That it is a beautiful consummation, we can sometimes see for ourselves, when we meet some aged person in whose life there is such a bright and sweet humanity, and true love, and restfulness, and grace, that we feel in their presence how a good old age must be desirable after such a life as all men are called to live in this stormy era, when, as the Psalm has it, "They mount up to heaven, and go down again to the depths, and their soul is melted because of trouble." Then "He maketh the storm a calm, and men are glad because they be quiet, so He bringeth them unto their desired haven." And we have all had to contrast an old age like that with another, in which there was no beauty which should cause us to desire it; restless, suspicious, hard, and graceless; that has never abandoned its sin, but has been abandoned of it, as the fire abandons burnt-out ashes; whose threescore and ten years' experience of the world has only gone to confirm their unbelief in it, while they still hug it, and dare not let it go, because when they peer with their poor, preoccupied eyes into the hereafter, they can only feel that "darkness, death, and long despair, reign in eternal silence there;" and when we ask what can make such a difference, we reach what I want especially to say, —

I. How to come to a good old age; and,

II. What then?

I. And this is to be first, and truly understood, an old age of any sort, is the result of the life I have lived, whatever that has been.

That above all outward seeming, or even inward feeling, is that solid, solemn sentence, "Whatsoever a man soweth, that shall he also reap." I can live so well, that at seventy earth and heaven together shall say, "I am such an one as Paul the aged." Yet from exceeding self-distrust, and want of the instant power to trust in God, I may not feel this at all, but look back on the way I have come, and say, "Better I had never been born than to live to so little purpose." Or I may shake at the impending change, at that other life into which the young *may* go soon, and I *must* go soon, and say, "I toil beneath the curse; but knowing not the universe, I fear to slide from this to worse." It is no matter what I feel, any more than it matters that a fruitful summer day shall gather a curtain of thick cloud about it as it sinks to rest, shutting out the shining heavens, and veiling all things in the mist. It has been a fruitful day all the same, and now the substance of it is in every grain of wheat, and in the heart of every apple within the zone, and its incense has gone into the heavens before it, so the fruitfulness abides, and its blessing rises, and the sun and moon would stand still, sooner than that should be lost.

On the other hand, my life may have been worthless as withered leaves, selfish and self-seeking since the day when I cheated my small schoolmate swapping marbles; hard to man, base to woman, abject to power, haughty to weakness, earthly, sensual, devilish. Yet, in my last days, the very selfishness that has been the ruling passion of my life, may lead me to grasp the delusion that another can bear my sin, and then lift me instantly into Paradise; and the good of feeling that the last bargain I have made, and the last advantage I have gained, is the best, may make me pass out of life, in the euthanasia of self-deception, into the pit. It is no matter what I feel, what I have done, if my life has been like that, it determines what I shall be. Angels, no more than men, "gather grapes of thorns, or figs of thistles;" and when they come to the gathering because the harvest is ripe, they will gather what there is.

There is one so-called religious tract, once in general circulation, and considered among the best, which seems to me to be blank blasphemy.

It is that remarkable narative written from what Burnet wrote of the last days of Wilmot, Earl of Rochester, the most profligate man, after his master, Charles II., of that era. He was an old man, through his vices, at thirty-four, and at the point of death was worn out utterly, and his mind was also much decayed, as his biographer says in the Encyclopædia. It was then that Burnet was called to see him, was attracted to him, as the result shows, partly by the pity of a noble heart, and partly by the hope of bringing so notorious a sinner (who was also an infidel and an earl) into the church. The result was, that he died, as it is believed, made clean through the atoning blood, and was taken straight to heaven, because our Protestantism leaves us no alternative but that or hell, and divides the places, and hopes and despairs of them, by a razor-edged dogma, this way and that.

Now let me never be suspected of trying to limit the infinite mercy. "O, praise the Lord, for he is good, for his mercy endureth forever." That Wilmot, Earl of Rochester, has been or will be saved, I doubt no more than I doubt my own existence. The ultimate fact I do not doubt;

the instant application of it, in that way, I utterly deny. What! make that man an angel of light, and clean from all sin, there and then, while women he had ruined were walking through London streets down to hell! set him singing at the foot of the great white throne, without a care, while mothers, whose daughters were lost through him, were weeping, heart-broken, in their blighted homes! when the whole life of England was baser because he had lived in it! when his poems and songs were only just starting out to sow their evil seeds through the long generations until now! I tell you that is blasphemy. "Whatsoever a man soweth, that shall he also reap," whether the harvest be gathered here or yonder. I get what I give. So, then, what I feel in my old age may be a very small matter. Wilmot was very happy; Luther, on the whole, was very miserable. He said, that rather than have much more of life, he would throw up his chance at Paradise, and felt every day, after he was fifty what such a one as Paul, the aged, meant, when he said, "We that are in this tabernacle do groan, being burdened." What I am, is the great thing; the feeling may answer to the fact or it may not;

that depends upon a great many matters that never disturb eternal verities at all.

Now, what I am from sixty to seventy, is the sum of what I have been from sixty back to sixteen. I have been getting together, letter by letter, and page by page, that which, good or bad, is now stereotyped, and stays so. Talking once with a friend who had been very sick, he told me that one remarkable fact in his sickness, while he was unconscious of all that went on about him, was the coming back of his life like a succession of pictures. Things that he had long forgotten, that were buried down deep in the past, came up again one by one, and were a part of himself. It was a dim intimation of what we have all been led to suspect from our own experience, — that things are not lost, but laid away, everything in its own place; and it is but another side of what I have tried to show you by a figure — our thoughts and deeds are the words and pages in the Book of Life. Slowly we gather them together, page by page, and when old age comes the story is told. Letters may be missing then, and words here and there obscure; but the whole meaning and spirit of it, the hardness and falsehood, or the tenderness and truth and love, the tenor and purpose of it, are then all to be read. It is noble or base. It will inspire or dishearten. It may be the life of a king like George the Fourth of England, in which there is not a line that the world would not gladly forget, or the life of a cobbler like John Pounds, who lived in the kingdom under that king, and out of his poverty lured with little gifts the poorest children in Plymouth to his small shanty, that he might teach them to read; and better things besides, giving his whole life for their salvation, whatever it be. I would not dare to say one word of old age before this, — that the most certain thing about it is, it is the solid result of a lifetime. It is no matter how we may feel who have to face it, that is what must abide at the heart of it, and be the warp and woof.

This brings me to say again, what may seem to have been left doubtful as I have tried to state this first thing, — that there is a line to be drawn, on the one side of which any man may look forward to an old age full of contentment, but on the other, if we take it, only of misery. It is that line which runs between what inspires the life and soul, and what merely exhausts it; what perishes in the doing or the using, and what abides forever; the fashion of this world that passes away, and the spirit of that which is as fresh and full forever, as the sea is of water, or the sun of fire.

There is a dull, heavy book I read sometimes, for one great lesson that I find in it — the Life of James Watt, the inventor of the steam engine. His life opened into sickness, and almost constant pain, and such heavy depression of the heart and mind, that when he was thirty-four, he writes, " I greatly doubt whether the silent mansion of the grave is not the happiest place." There, we naturally say, if he do not die young, or get into his nature some vast compensation of religious feeling, is the making of a miserable old man; or, even if he be religious, he may become one of that unhappy number we are always meeting, who has a great deal of religion, but no rest. Well, Scott met him in a company when he was in his eighty-second year, and wondered at his cheerful presence, and how he was at home with everybody about him, talking to every one in a select company of the best men in Scotland with the keenest interest in what interested that particular man. Jeffrey had seen him a year before, and says he never saw him in his life more animated, instructive, and delightful. Campbell passed a day with him when he was nearly eighty-three, and says, " It was one of the most amusing and instructive days of my whole life." Another writes of this time, that he was telling a Swedish artist how to make the best brushes for painting, and this lady how to cure her smoky chimney, and that one how to obtain fast colors for her dresses, and teaching a child how to play on the jews-harp, and how to make a dulcimer, and was altogether an inexhaustible fountain of interest and instruction to all that came to him, and only distressed and uneasy when anybody insisted on reminding him what a mighty work he had done in his long lifetime.

Now, I ask what made this vast alteration between James Watt at thirty-four and at eighty-three, and hear some such answer as this: James Watt did dutifully what God set him to do on this earth, not caring so much for the profit or the praise his deed might bring, as that the work should be well done. That was one thing. The other was, that what he did, though it was only the perfecting of the steam engine, he wrought for a pure purpose of God, and for the the help of humanity. It was a part of that great plan, of which the Gospel of Jesus Christ is the perfect crown — the glory of God and the salvation of men. That glory was only made greater by the application of steam, through law, to machinery; and humanity was only blessed by the lifting away of one of its burdens. But it was a divine work, in its degree, and it brought a divine reward. So the dutiful life, through sickness, depression, and pain, brought a restful and noble old age, into which, while one by one his old friends left him, and he felt his own feet touch the chill of the great river, the consolations of God came pouring plentifully, banished all fear, and made him feel, as one has said, how "age is but the shadow of death, cast where he standeth in the radiant path of immortality."

And this is the preparation for a good old age: Duty well done, for its own sake, for God's sake, and for the sake of the commonwealth of man. When a man works only for himself, he gets neither rest here, nor reward hereafter. When I work for myself, and live for myself, I exhaust myself; but when I work for others, wisely and well, I work for God too; and for my work I get that bread which cometh down from heaven. And duty can find an infinite outcome. It can nurse a sick child, or teach a healthy one. It can be John Pounds or John Milton. It can found the firms and factories, that are the roots of civilization, and the schools and churches and libraries, that are its life's blood. In all these ways, and all others, the preparation for a good old age is my duty unselfishly done, trusting in God, and living purely.

II. I said, when old age comes, what then? The preparation for it is a pure life, and faithfulness to duty now. What comfort and advantage can come to it, and abide through it, until I die! If I may take such instances as I have met with in life, or in books, or have thought of as possible, I want, when I come to be an old man, to feel and to act something like this: First of all, I will try to make the best of it; not the best of what is bad at the best, as some seem to think, but of what is, if I will but understand it, the best of my whole life, because it is the last.

So that, if I should be favored then to feel clear and strong, and this organism, through which the spirit works, shall serve me, I will remember what good there was at eighty-three in a man like James Watt, and how Solon said that after sixty a man was not worth much, but himself lived to be over fourscore for all that, and at fourscore did the very best work of his life. I will then muster with these all the grand old men, away back to such a one as Paul the aged, whose age has brought its own peculiar power, and made the world glad they were spared so long to be such a blessing, and so I will keep on as they did, not permitting my best friend to cheat me out of the count of my years because I am still active, but will carry it all to the account and the advantage of my old age, and the blessing that may abide in that.

But if it be otherwise, and long before I have to go through the river the eye grows dim, and the fires abate, and a grasshopper becomes a burden, and the tramp a shuffle, and I have the grace to see, what people may be too kind to say, that my active days are over, and I had better have done; then I will try to see also how this is the best that can happen, because it is the kind, good Master taking out of my hand the hammer I were otherwise loath to lay down, and putting out the fire, in which I should only potter, and waste material, and saying to me, in this good, wise way, "Now sit down a while, until it is time to go. You have wrought long enough. Rest and be quiet." And then, please God, I will not break out into that shameful lamenting I have heard from old men, about "the tender light of a day that is gone, that can never come back to me, and powers and appetites withered away."

Perhaps, even, I will rise so high as to thank God it is so, and that the passions and appetites I have had to watch like wild beasts sometimes, are tamed at last, and I am free to be, in some poor measure, as the angels of God. I do think, indeed, that such outcries as we hear and read about the blight that comes to age in the loss of its powers, are as unreasonable and unpardonable as anything that can be thought of. I can think of nothing now that I shall more earnestly desire when, as Paul the aged said, "the outward man perishes," than that the inward man should be so renewed, day by day, as to make me feel there is no loss, but a gain, in that, because "there is a building of God, a house not made with hands, eternal in the heavens," where mortality shall be swallowed up of life.

Then another thing which I want to be sure about, when that time comes, is, that the world is not rushing headlong into destruction because I am no longer guiding it. It may be cause, or it may be effect, I can never quite tell which; but I have noticed it is one of the keenest miseries of a restless old age, that it is quite convinced everything is going wrong, and getting worse and worse, from the little grandchild, who is not at all what his grandfather was seventy years ago, to the vast and solemn interests of the nation, going, beyond redemption, to ruin. It was this which made that misery in Luther's later life, of which I have spoken. He was sure the world was given over to the Evil One. His last letters speak of life as utterly hopeless. "The world," he said, "is bent on going to the devil." "It is like a drunken peasant." "Put him on his horse on one side, and he tumbles over on the other; take him in whatever way you will, you cannot help him." Now, the evil with Luther dated back many years before this, when he would not trust our common humanity in as reasonable a request as it ever made, but took the side of the nobles against the peasants, and with his own hand tried to put back the clock of the Reformation.

It is one of the qualities of the most restful and joyful old age, that it believes in the perpetual incoming of the kingdom of our God and of his Christ. And so its heart is full of belief and hope in the new time and the new generation. "The former times," such old men say, "were not better than these, and I was not better than my grandson." Like Paul the aged, such an old age is not sure it shall see the coming kingdom and power and glory, but it is sure it is to come, so that infancy is to it a perpetual prophecy; and the old man can always take the young babe, and cry, "Lord, now lettest thou thy servant depart in peace, according to thy word; for mine eyes have seen thy salvation." It is one of the best blessings of a good old age, that it can believe in a good new age which it has helped to bring in, and in which it is permitted to stay for a little while, and welcome it. Such a one as Paul the aged is always quiet about that. Then I shall hope to realize how wonderful is this great, faithful Providence, which, since I can first remember, has wrought such marvels in the earth; how men and nations are in the hand of God. And while age will make my religious ideas so unalterable that, if one shall come as directly from God as Christ did, with a new Gospel, I shall not be able to give up this for that, I shall be able to feel that all the differences of good, true men are included within the great harmonies of God.

But all this, and all else, can only come in one way. In a wise little book, given me lately, on the art of prolonging life, the author says that in old age the system should have more generous nourishment. It is the correlative of a truth about the soul. Say what we will, —

> " Except we are growing pure and good,
> There can be no good in growing old. ·
> It is a path we would fain avoid if we could;
> And it means growing ugly, suspicious, and cold."

God help us if, as we are growing older we do not grow better, and do not nourish our souls on the most generous thoughts and aspirations.

A noble German thinker speaks of his intention to store up, for his death-day, whatever is best in all he has thought and read. I would not wait for that day. I would have my store ready, when, some time after sixty, I begin to feel the first chill of the cold waters, and then feed my heart on it all the way along to the end. The great promises of the sacred books, the faith in the fatherhood that was in Christ, the joyful hope that rings through great poems, like that of Wordsworth on Immortality, and Tennyson's "In Memoriam," and this wonderful work of "Jean Paul" which I have just mentioned. Then the winter of my life shall not be the winter of my discontent. I will take a lesson even from the little creatures that hide in the woods, that in bright summer weather make their store-house, and in the autumn lay up their store; then, when the storms sweep through their sylvan homes, and the frost and snow turn the great trees into pillars of ice, live snug and warm among their kind, and wait for the new spring.

> "Grow old, then, cheerily;
>   The best is yet to be
> The last of life, for which the first was made.
>
> "Our times are in His hand,
>   Who saith, A whole I planned;
>   Youth shows but half trust —
>   God sees all;
>   Nor be afraid."

XVI.

AT THE SOLDIERS' GRAVES.

Isa. lxi. 3: "Beauty for ashes."

We gather, to-day, from our great city, in this city of the dead, for a noble purpose. It is, that the tender grace may rest on us that rests on the dust of the men who died to save us; and that we may strew flowers on their graves, not so much for a token that we will not forget them, as for a sign that they may not forget us.

It is a good time to meet for this purpose just as the spring is passing into summer, and the full bloom of the world is about us, to make this the symbol of the feeling that is in our hearts for those who went forth as spring was opening into summer in their lives, and gave them to their country.

And this fitness in the time is the more fitting from the fact that this day falls on a Sunday. It is the first time we have come together in this fashion for this great purpose. It gives another grace to the rite, that it should be done on a day set apart for sacred things. I am glad of the beautiful coincidence. It makes the day to me still more sacred. Indeed, I cannot but feel that it would be a vast advantage if the time we give to this sacrament of the flowers could always be a Sunday. If on this holy day we could close our churches with one consent all over the land, gather in the cemeteries where these heroes rest, and hold great services of psalm and prayer, with only the arches of heaven for the dome of our temple, then we should have a service that all would be glad to attend, a church from which none would feel excluded, and such a blessing as seldom comes to little synagogues, where we meet for more private devotion.

But simply touching this as something that I devoutly hope may come to pass, for the good of the church and the commonwealth alike, I cannot but feel that better still than the time is the spirit that brings us together and makes us one, as if in this great multitude there is one common heart. It is not possible that in the common reaches of life, there should not be a vast difference in the thought and feeling of a multitude like this. I think it best there should be. The dead levels of uniformity on most of the questions that come home to us, are the lurking-places of malarias, and only the mountain ranges of diversity are the fastnesses of health. But as on this summer Sunday the sun draws this whole green world to look up and to drink in his light and fire, so the glory that burns and shines in the deeds of the men who are resting here, and all over the land, and in the sea, draws us as the sun draws the world; and as these men were made one in that cause for which they gave their life, we are made one in our loyalty to their dust. When we come here,— though we have never seen the face of one buried beneath these mounds,— we gather about the graves of our brothers and sons. When the youth left his home and his mother to defend his country, he was adopted by the whole motherhood of the republic, and every home made him one of its own. So we cast the flowers on the graves of our kindred; and from this low, green hill, our hearts yearn over the dust of all brave soldiers who fought and fell. It is a consecration that reaches wherever a man is laid whose heart beat for the mighty work God gave us to do in this generation. One great, simple article was their whole creed,— that the American Republic, just as it was then, was good enough to live, and fight, and die for. It is good enough, as we gather here, to make us forget all minor things in their noble sacrifice, and in our thankfulness to God for raising up such men. They died that we might live. They gave their life a ransom for many. So it is well that we should have but one heart as we meet about their graves, and speak of their great devotion.

It has seldom been my lot, in all the years of my ministry, to feel so entirely unequal to any work I have had to do, as I do to-day. As I have thought of the great honor in your request that I should address you, I could not but feel it was all a mistake to select such a man as I am for this work. It is one of the touching things that have come to us from the old time, that when a man wanted to move a great multitude to do some piece of grace, he stood before them and held up a poor stump, from which the hand had gone in defence of their homes. He said no word; he simply bared the maimed limb, and in a moment the multitude was lifted into the grace he sought. So I have thought you had better have done to-day: not to take me, or any man like me, whose work in the strife for which these men fell was so poor and thin, but to take one of your own veterans, a man who, when the trumpet called our nation to battle, went out and stood fast, fighting for the land; who endured hardness like a good soldier, until the war was ended, and then, coming back, quietly took his place as a citizen, doing his duty with the smart of his old wounds about him, but never complaining, or thinking that God had given him the harder lot. Such a man might stand mute, or simply say, "These are the graves of my comrades," and then no speech that could be made by the tongue of man beside would ever touch us with an eloquence like that. One mute appeal from a maimed arm, pointed down at these green mounds, if we had eyes to see what the appeal meant, would cover these graves deeper with summer blossoms than they have ever been covered with winter snows. Soldiers of the Republic, you cannot suspect what power abides in your broken bodies and shed blood, to shake the heart of every true American. That was the power you should have seized for this great occasion. I went to the battle-field; you fought on it. I nursed and tended in steamboat and hospital; but you wrestled with the agonies of wounds I could not feel. God knows my heart was always full of sympathy; but that could not underreach your pain. All the tales of old heroism I had ever read faded out in the face of your quiet endurance; and you taught me new lessons of what a man can do, when God helps him, in any strife. The grandest sights I shall ever see on this earth I saw in your camps and hospitals. It is only my resolution, sacred, I trust, as my life, never to refuse the request of a soldier, that has held me up to stand here, and try to speak to you by the graves of your comrades. My advantage, as I do try, rests in the infinite eloquence of your mere presence. I fall back on your reserves.

Mine is the description; yours, the demonstration. I can only tell the things that you and yours have done.

And so it cannot be my business, in the light of this confession, to catalogue these deeds as the substance of my poor discourse. They stand in their own strength, and are enshrined in a glory to which my words can add no lustre. Neither can I pretend to touch any lesson for those that have taken part in these great transactions. So long as the chaplain falls back while the soldier fights the battle, I think there is very little room for the chaplain to talk to the soldier, either of duty or glory. I was at the rear when you were at the front what time the thunders and fires of the battle shook the common heart. I will not pretend to come to the front, and let you pass to the rear now, when the battle is over.

But beside the soldier to-day stands the citizen, and I have thought that if I could speak from the soldier to the citizen, I should do all that may become a man in my position. If I can do that, I shall be content.

I want to catch the spirit, if I can, of that

great time in which the soldier took the first place, to feel, through its lurid and terrible infoldings, for the divine soul that was in it from first to last. Within a few years the chemist has found the sweetest dye of heaven in that crude oil which springs out of the dark and dismal deeps of the earth. This true transcript of the sky was born in the heart of that darkness. So there is, if we have the wisdom to find it, the light of heaven at the heart of this old trouble through which we have come. And I think we shall find it, if we consider three things that touch us, naturally, as we think of the men whose dust is buried beneath these mounds, and is rising and blending with the glory about us,—that they, and all like them everywhere, were:—

I. The true heroes.
II. The true patriots.
III. The true saviours of this land.

I mention the hero first to mark my sense of the fact that of these three great things, always to be found in the true citizen-soldier, this with all its wonderful grace, is the least and lowest, and in the strife of which these graves are mute, but most eloquent witnesses, no man will more readily testify than the soldier himself who hears me, it was the common quality found on both sides. This, indeed, was deeply to be desired, if such a contest was inevitable as that through which we have come. Now that two hundred years have gone, and all the old soreness has gone with the years, the Englishman is proud of the splendid heroism displayed by Puritan and Cavalier alike, and would not, for any price, have it possible that half the great family, when the quarrel came to the solemn arbitration of the sword, should turn out poltroons and cowards. And while it was essential that the Puritan should win in the last battle, — as it always is that heaven should win against hell, — the heroism of those who stood for the wrong is still the grand background to the picture of Ironside and Roundhead standing for the right. They had to come together when the old war was over, and band together for the common good. They could only do that as they felt that each had sterling qualities of heroism which the other was bound to respect. So it is with us to-day, and will be forever. When the old bitterness has gone out of our hearts, and all the wounds are healed, and we are one nation, we shall be proud of the heroic qualities displayed by so many on the other side, and feel that this heroism is the common possession of the men of our stock. North or South, it makes no difference as to that. Right or wrong, that grand quality abides, and, like the fallen angels in Milton's mighty epic, such traits come out, even in their struggle with the Lord of Hosts, as fill us with a sorrowful respect for such natures, while we utterly condemn the sin that dragged them down.

Now we are coming together. We shall come together; and then when the old pain has gone out, it will be better for us all, and for all the world, that there should be men like Stonewall Jackson on the other side. For Fort Pillow, and Lawrence, and Andersonville, and the Libby, and all such murder and torture, I feel an unutterable loathing. Such things can only be done by the very spawn and refuse of the pit. To be concerned in them, by implication even, is to be blotted out of the book of American life; but heroism, like this that I speak about, knew nothing of that; and heroism, I say, was a common quality. A fairer light rests this day on the graves of these heroes because they fell fighting with heroes in battle. And they will one day be friends worthy of our friendship, who were foes worthy of our steel. Our President has done no wiser thing than when, that morning lately, his great antagonist came to see him, soldier to soldier, face to face, he gave him precedence of all the vampires that were seeking some way by which they might fasten on the body politic, and fill their veins from its life. He simply gave precedence to his foe, who wanted now to be a friend, over those that, in the guise of friendship, are to-day the worst foes the country has to encounter.

This, then, is the first truth: we deck the graves of heroes, all the more heroic in that they had to meet their peers in heroism, and conquer them. Dearly, then, we can treasure all beside that brings this noble quality home to our hearts; can watch them leave their homes, while mothers, and sisters, and wives gather about them, not to hinder, thank God, but to help, — Spartan women, with Christian hearts, battling with their tears, only giving their prayers free course, and their words of deep courage, until the boys were out of sight.

We can think of them in their camps, bracing up their hearts to the strange, new life, with that distant look in their eyes I have seen so many times, telling me the spirit is not there. It has swept over the distance between the tent and the homestead, and is looking in, and watching the life that must go on in its steady round, whether the husband or brother is present or absent.

Then, as the day darkens, we can watch them go forth to battle — to that awful work which seems at once to touch the direct and divinest possibilities of life; set themselves sternly, shoulder to shoulder, make their breasts a bulwark for their motherland; to die if they must, or be maimed if they must, but to conquer whatever comes: and then if it is to die, to depart, as I have seen so many go, as when God kissed his servant on the mountain, and he slept. No complaint, and no fear; only the one great assurance that always comes with the well-done — the assurance that all is well here and yonder; that a life is always good for a life; no fear for the soul that has done its duty; only the day-dawn of an infinite hope.

It has been my lot to kneel at the death-bed of many Christians. I never knelt by one on which the light from Heaven shone quite so clear as it did on the poor cot of some soldiers who could not tell me much about their faith, but could tell me all I wanted to know about their duty. Dear, tender, beautiful souls, speaking of the wife and children with their last breath, and of their hope that the country for which they died would not forget them, and then leaving all the rest to God. No matter about the harp and crown; if that was not best, they were not going to lament. So far they were sure of their footing, and they did not fear for the next step. To die for the great Mother was enough — that they felt was, in their poor measure, as when Christ died for their race. Heroes! No better or brighter heroism was ever seen on this planet, than that which shone forth from these men, to whose dust we bring this beauty, wherever they lie.

I said, just now, that heroism was the lowest of the three grand qualities by which these risen souls, that look down on us to-day, are forever to be distinguished. It may be for the reason that it is the quality on which the others must rest, and but for which they could have no real existence. The hero underlies the patriot and the saviour. Patriotism and sacrifice rest on the quaking sand, when heroism, the unconquerable quality, does not hold them up. "First win the battle, then look after me," Colonel Silas Miller cried. It was the instinct of the hero. Heroism, Carlyle has said, is that divine relation which, in all times, relates a great man to other men. It unites us to-day to every hero, in the land and in the sea, who fell for our country. But for their deeds we should have no country; the heroes of the Nation, alive and dead, are at the foundation of the American nationality.

II. I said that above the hero stands the patriot. I speak still of the soldier when I say this, because it is the lesson of his life I am touching; and he is greater as a patriot than a hero, because he rose above all minor things, and gave himself, without reservation, to the republic.

I mean no offence when I say that there is a sectional patriotism, just as there is a sectarian Christianity. I say it the more freely, because I have to confess that I belong to a section in the republic and a sect in the church, and I cannot see my way out of my limitations. In ordinary times, I have said already, I believe this to be best. It is the disagreement of the atmospheres that cleanses the air. Our stormy lake there is infinitely better than the Dead Sea. The only perfect repose I know of is the awful stillness of the grave. We can never cease contending about principles and policies of government; and all honest contention, loyal still to the land, is like the systole and diastole of a true heart.

But when the crisis came that was to test the heroism of these men, it was to test their patriotism too. We were in a mighty contention among ourselves. We were not clear about our duty; to many a man who fought and fell for us, there came a time, in those days, when the reason for standing back, and substantially deserting the country, must have been as subtle and strong as the reasons for deserting Jehovah, in the old war in heaven, were to many a still unfallen angel. But in that moment, when our sole hope of salvation, under God, was in the compacted strength of every true man, then, as in Switzerland once, every canton poured out its people, and from every mountain came the mountaineer, to strike one stroke,— and the land was saved. So these men passed over the lines of difference, to stand shoulder to shoulder: forgetting the old battle-cries of the party, they gave themselves, without reserve, for the land; and it was this that made them greater than heroes. They could be heroes on the wrong side; they could only be patriots on the right side. Above all the reasons that could be given why they should hold back, and let "Mene, Tekel" be written, once for all, across our history, rose this one thing that could not be reasoned about,— the salvation of the land. It was to them as when you shall give a man reasons for not helping his mother; but then she shall say, "My son, I am your mother. I suckled you at my breast, and held you on my knees." Then that is enough; there is no reason that can meet that instinct; it lifts the man with a mighty spring to stand by her side.

This was the patriotism of these men. They forgot everything but the one great tender tie. "Let us agree to have a country," they said, "and then we can afford to differ about the best way to take care of it." They counted all things as loss save the excellency of the glory of an unbroken republic. And so it was natural that citizens of Chicago should think very tenderly, at such a time as this, of one who rests alone at the other extreme of our city. He was a soldier, though he struck no stroke except the stroke of his mighty words. He died just as the trumpet was sounding for the host, but he died fighting with a mighty ardor for the land he loved. I cast my poor blossom across the grave of Douglas, who, when the crisis came against which he had always striven by the best light he had, knew nothing under heaven but the undivided land.

Out of the graves of our heroes, everywhere, blooms this fair flower of patriotism. True men, who could rise above all minor things to the height of this great argument, that the republic, just as it was then, trembling, seemingly on the verge of dissolution, was good enough to live and die for, so lived and died for the republic; and now they abide in the unfading splendor of hero and patriot together, as we abide a moment in their shining presence, to adorn their graves.

III. There is one step higher still these great

souls have taken, — the loftiest men can ever attain to in this mortal life: they are not only our heroes and patriots, as they stand there above us in their shining ranks, but the saviours of their country, and of all that was bound up in her undivided destiny!

When I try to weigh the whole matter which called these men, at last, to their great estate, I am forced to the conclusion that there was no way left to save this nation but by its most precious blood. God sent prophets and teachers, as great and good as he ever sent to any nation, and they poured out their hearts for us, — and it was all in vain. Everything was done which could be done, short of this shedding of blood, to avert the woe; but we were helpless to avert it. Only the noblest and best we had, leaping into the gulf in his best estate, could close the chasm, and secure the integrity of the land. Indeed, if this were the time and place, it would not be hard to tell how the trumpet that sounded the war did but announce the end of a truce; and this struggle was only a new outbreak of the long fight between despotic and democratic institutions, in which Gettysburg was made one with Marston-

Moor. No such thing can be done to-day. It is enough to say the solemn crisis came in which the best we could have, could only be obtained at the cost of the best we had. Then these men came forward,— young men, with the bloom on their lives, strong men, and true,— the best we had, and offered themselves, if that would do, as the price of the national salvation. Budding hopes were in the heart of the youth, of a fair home by and by, and a good wife to keep it, and gracious presences fresh from God to people it, and a career burdened with the blessing that comes to every true man in this noble country. But he gave it all for the land, and said, "Live or die, that shall be my first care."

Strong ties bound others,— home, wife, children, fortune, a career already open,— everything the heart could wish. To give up life at thirty was nothing beside giving up these things that life had brought. "My ten great reasons for taking no risk," one said, "were a wife and nine children."

I have no standard by which to measure what the men who left these things, and rest in these graves, have done. It seems like trying to measure the infinite. The infinite is in it. But there they stood in that great day,— the youth in the portals of his life, the man at his fireside,— and they looked right into the heart of all that was about them, and before them, and above them; and then they said, "I can give it all if my country needs it." Then they went out and gave it all for the need. They kept nothing back; like brave Captain Thompson, they said, "I leave all with God;" like Colonel Wright, when one arm was gone, they could "thank God that one hand might guide a horse;" like Major Chandler, they said, "Where I can be of most service I will stay;" like Silas Miller, they shouted, as their life leaped out, "First win the battle, then look after me;" like Mulligan, they cried, "I am dying, boys; but don't lose the colors;" and like Ransom, they said, "I have tried to do my duty, and have no fear for myself after death."

Do I mention these men, whose words still sound in our ears, it is only to realize for you the truth about all these noble dead. Not one soldier, I care not how obscure, giving his life in this fashion, falls short of this great place — not one such man has died in vain. It is a whole sacrifice, and they are all saviours. They stand above us this day, as we stand by their graves, risen and glorified. I question the value of no other sacrifice; but this, to me, is the greatest — the price that was paid for our nationality in the true gold of their true life. Nothing can rise above that, except that help of God, without which all were vain. Glorious forever, with the hero and patriot, stands the saviour. All that a man has he will give for his life. Yet these gave their life, asking for nothing again, but that their land and nation might not be torn asunder.

I have been led to make this threefold distinction in the glory of our dead, because I have felt it would not only give us a clearer conception of the true nature of what they have done, but might come home the more weightily to those of us who stand here to-day. Heroism, patriotism, and the great office of the saviour, are the threefold cord that must still bind every true American to his duty, and open the way to his greatest place. We must be heroes still, and patriots, and saviours, or we must stand in the shadow, while these men stand in the light, and be content to be despised when they are worshipped. God gives no man a supreme place who will not do a supreme work. War and peace are but the two ways that he has marked out for the one thing. Heroism as high, patriotism as precious, and a saviourship as sacred as that which these men rose to, are still open to you and me. Pre-emption from any one of these glorious qualities is pre-emption from the best that God has to give. To be hero, patriot, and saviour is the mark of the prize of our high calling. To fight against corruption, as these fought against conspiracy; to stand for the whole land, in peace, as they did in war; and in war, if it come again, to make the uttermost sacrifice which can be demanded for the commonwealth of America,— these are just as truly the demand made on you and me as was the demand on the men whose dust moulders beneath these mounds. The body and blood of this sacrament of flowers for the heroes and patriots and saviours of our land, are lost to our life, if they fail to make us heroes, patriots, and saviours also.

I must not weary you. I have but a few more words that insist on being said. Brave men, I have said; good soldiers,— and you gather from this the idea that I have meant men, and not women, — but I could never hope to pardon myself, let alone be pardoned of God and my country, if I failed to speak at such a time of the woman, too, and of the woman, in every respect, as the exemplar of the great qualities I have pointed out in the man. The woman stood as truly as the man by this great cause; made her sacrifice as quietly and as perfectly as he did, and on the battle-field, or in the hospital, or the house, was the hero, the patriot, and the saviour, too.

When the youth would look into the eyes of the maiden for confirmation of his longing to let his love of the land take precedence of his love for her, she said Amen, gave him the kiss of consecration, and sent him forth, her true knight. When the husband said, with a shaking voice, to the wife, "I feel almost as if I ought to go, and leave you and the children," the voice of the wife grew steady as she said, "Go, then;" turning almost into altogether, in the sacrifice; and she looked on with steady eyes, at least until he was gone, because all the courage there was, or could be, must be taken with him to the camp. Then, as the work went on, and grew ever more dreadful, and new drafts were made on her life for help to the sick and wounded, and for everything that a woman can do to cube the might of man, with unflinching steadiness she toiled and suffered; supplying, with a measureless generosity, everything that was needed to the call; sanctifying this very day, this Sunday of ours, O, so many times, by doing all manner of work, and doing everything, not merely without a murmur, — for that we might have expected of her patience and her love, — but doing it with a mighty cheerfulness, that sent cheer into every hero's soul, and was the expression, through all the darkness, of the light she foresaw and foretold, — singing of the coming of victory and peace, when the full price was paid, and the powers of darkness were driven away by the power of the living God.

Under thousands of mounds, in the circle of our land this day, rest these true women, heroes, patriots, and saviours, with the men. Broken down at their tasks, when the poor frame could hold the great soul no longer, they died, as they had lived, for the motherland; not having received the promise, but seeing it afar off, and with their last breath praying for the establishment of the right. Over all these graves we cast our blossoms, as we cast them on the graves of our noble men. These flowers, and that which these flowers symbolize everywhere, we cast on the graves in which all women are resting, whose souls are risen to that great place, and stand with the angels of God.

Neither can I forget, as I stand here, that company of unknown martyrs who never found their way where they could fight for the right, yet could not countenance the wrong, and so were slain, and buried beneath the ruins of their own homesteads, and lie there to-day under the Southern sun. Poor, dumb, nameless martyrs — men and women who could only suffer, but had no chance to do, or could only do in nooks and corners, carrying their lives in their hands; and then, at last, giving them for the land that was never to know their name. Not one such grave of man or woman, white or black, can be left out of this consecration. They did what they could; we give for it what we have. They need nothing we can do; we need to feed our hearts on their great lesson of how good it is to be steadfast and true, all to yourself, if the host is on the other side, and to die one lone man or woman for the right, where the wrong seems supreme. My heart goes out, as I stand here this day, to those nameless graves of the nameless martyrs. I bid you remember them as you offer your gift. They, too, are our kinsmen and friends: they died that we might live.

Finally, I bid you look with a tender pity on the graves of those who died fighting against us, if they knew no better. They know better now, and if they could come back into life, would be with us and of us. It was the fate of many, more than their fault, to be drawn into that dreadful vortex, to fight against the holiest things, and think they were doing God service. It is their doom to have fallen fighting for the wrong. Let us cast the mantle of forgiveness over their graves, and let some poor blossom overflow that way as a token of what we feel. We alone can afford to forgive and forget. We cannot afford to wait until those forgive and forget who are at our mercy. O, strong, and true, and tender is the North! and this is the time for tenderness.

And then, as these great thanksgivings well up in our souls, and we say, God bless the land that has been saved by this sacrifice! let us do what these great ones are beseeching us to do from their high place — thank God for making them what they are. Then, as the starshine pales before the sunshine, the light of the glory of God will flood these cemeteries, set shining ones beside all the graves, and send us home with a sense that we have seen only the grave-clothes. All our dead are risen! Death is swallowed up in Victory!

ROBERT COLLYER'S WORKS.

I.
NATURE AND LIFE.

TENTH EDITION.

Price $1.50. Fine edition, bevelled boards, gilt edges, with *fac-simile* of Mr. Collyer's Autograph stamped in Gold, and a View of his early Home. Price, $2.00. Sent by mail on receipt of the price.

OPINIONS OF THE PRESS.

The broad humanity of the writer, his ready sympathy, his recognition of the superiority of true religion over all its forms, and last, but not least, the poetic quality of his thought, bespeak for him a hearing with all earnest men. As much as Mr. Beecher, he belongs to all the sects. — *The Nation, New York.*

Their peculiar charm is to be found in the freshness and glow of their sympathy with all human conditions. — *Independent, New York.*

Every page is bright with good cheer, and presents considerations that are calculated to strengthen the best motives, lead to the noblest living, and inspire the heart with child-like trust in the Infinite Father. — *The Liberal Christian.*

The result of Mr. Collyer's self-education, and consequent original style of thought, is manifest in these sermons. Healthiness is the term which may most properly be applied to them. There are no signs of dyspepsia or bronchitis in them. You may be sure his lungs are sound, his chest broad, his arm strong, his head clear. They fairly glow with the ruddiness of fresh, out-door health. Their tone is always manly and sincere, and expression clear, concise, and convincing. — *Chicago Tribune.*

No thoughtful man or woman can read these sermons without gaining good thereby, — without having the heart set aflame by the love of God, and nature, and man, which is revealed in musical simplicity in every line thereof. — *Republican, Chicago.*

The themes are drawn from the every-day experience of life; from the hopes, the sorrows, the perplexities, the aspirations of the human heart, and are treated with a wisdom, a gentleness, a pathos, a rich, loving sympathy, which raise them above the usual sphere of eloquence into that of persuasive and touching counsel. — *New York Tribune.*

All of them are aglow with a sweet, fresh, spiritual life, that sheds a radiance of hope, and faith, and love on the darkest theme. Some of them are more than sermons, — they are poems, rich in thought and beautiful in expression. — *Portland Transcript.*

Happy the man to whom these sermons — these poems, rather, for such in very truth they are — come in his hour of need. They will help him over many of the rough places of his life; and when we put them on our shelves, it shall not be side by side with other sermons, but Longfellow and Tennyson shall keep them company on either hand. — *Christian Examiner.*

Sermons though these are, they set every page ablaze, and make the book as entertaining to a reader of taste and wholesome moral sympathies as a romance of Scott or a drama of Shakespeare. — *Freewill Baptist Quarterly.*

II.
A MAN IN EARNEST:
LIFE OF A. H. CONANT.

Price $1.25.
Fine edition, with Portrait of Mr. Conant, price $2.00.

To such as would have the most attractive bit of biography of the day, we commend "A Man in Earnest," with the assurance that their estimate of the value of life will be enlarged, strengthened, and purified thereby; and, if they do not rise with the belief that Mr. Conant was the wisest of men, they will be sure that Robert Collyer is the most charming and appreciative of biographers. — *Evening Post, Chicago.*

Those who have read his "Nature and Life," as well as those who have heard him speak, will read the book, not so much to learn the story of Mr. Conant's life, as to come in contact once more with the fresh, earnest eloquence, the noble, genial, inspiring sentiments, the large heart of Mr. Collyer. It is the prerogative of genius to glorify with song, or eloquence, or wondrous touch whatever subject it treats; and so this gentle though brave and manly life of a pioneer preacher is set before us a *genre* picture, made glorious and beautiful and powerful by the strong and radiant touches of a master hand. To know the writer is to be magnetized and charmed by him; to read this little book will be to enjoy and be elevated by it. — *Worcester Gazette.*

III.
THE LIFE THAT NOW IS.

With an excellent Steel Portrait of the Author, engraved by Perine.
Price, $1.50.
Fine edition, bevelled boards, gilt edges, price $2.00.

A new volume, by Robert Collyer, of Chicago, is announced by Horace B. Fuller, of Boston. That it will be a treasury of wisdom and wit, of the most delicate insight, the most humane sympathy, the most poetic imagination, all who have heard the eloquent preacher, or read his delightful "Nature and Life," will be sure. — GEORGE WILLIAM CURTIS, *in Harper's Weekly.*

Mr. Fuller expects to publish a second series of sermons by Robert Collyer. "Nature and Life" has sold towards ten thousand copies; the forthcoming book will doubtless have a still larger sale, for the enviable fame of Mr. Collyer has grown very fast of late years, and there are hundreds of thousands now of the most intelligent persons between the Atlantic and the Rocky Mountains who prize his golden words, and yet more the vast heart that he puts into all he says. He breathes on dead phrases, and they become living souls. — *Boston Correspondence of Cincinnati Chronicle.*

Rev. Robert Collyer, who is another instance of a rare poetic genius appearing in an English workingman, who is indeed one of the rarest prose poets the English race has produced, will soon issue another book. His theology is unsound, doubtless; but his poetry and his human sympathy are unsurpassed. — *New York Independent.*

HORACE B. FULLER, Publisher,
14 BROMFIELD ST., BOSTON.

THEODORE PARKER'S WRITINGS.
NEW EDITION.

A DISCOURSE OF MATTERS PERTAINING TO RELIGION. Fourth Edition. 1 vol. 12mo, cloth. $1.50.

I. Of Religion in General; or, The Religious Element and Its Manifestations.
II. Relation of the Religious Element to God; or, A Discourse of Inspiration.
III. Relation of the Religious Element to Jesus of Nazareth; or, A Discourse of Christianity.
IV. Relation of the Religious Element to the Greatest of Books; or, A Discourse of the Bible.
V. Relation of the Religious Element to the Greatest of Human Institutions; or, A Discourse of the Church.

SERMONS OF THEISM, ATHEISM, AND THE POPULAR THEOLOGY. 1 vol. 12mo, cloth. $1.50.

Introduction.
I. Speculative Atheism regarded as a Theory of the Universe.
II. Practical Atheism regarded as a Principle of Ethics.
III. The Popular Theology of Christendom regarded as a Theory of the Universe.
IV. The Popular Theology of Christendom regarded as a Principle of Ethics.
V. Speculative Theism regarded as a Theory of the Universe.
VI. Practical Theism regarded as a Principle of Ethics.
VII. The Function and Influence of the Idea of Immortal Life.
VIII. The Universal Providence of God.
IX., X. The Economy of Pain and Misery under the Universal Providence of God.

TEN SERMONS OF RELIGION. 1 vol. 12mo, cloth. $1.50.

I. Piety, and Its Relation to Manly Life.
II. Truth and the Intellect.
III. Justice and the Conscience.
IV. Love and the Affections.
V. Conscious Religion and the Soul.
VI. The Culture of the Religious Powers.
VII. Conscious Religion as a Source of Strength.
VIII. Conscious Religion as a Source of Joy.
IX. Conventional and Natural Sacraments.
X. Communion with God.

ADDITIONAL SPEECHES, ADDRESSES, AND OCCASIONAL SERMONS. 2 vols. 12mo, cloth. $3.00.

VOL. I.
I. Speech at the Ministerial Conference in Boston, May 29, 1851.
II. The Boston Kidnapping, — the Rendition of Thomas Sims.
III. The Aspect of Freedom in America.
IV. Discourse occasioned by the Death of Daniel Webster.
V. The Nebraska Question.
VI. The Condition of America in Relation to Slavery.

VOL. II.
I. The Progress of America.
II. The New Crime against Humanity, — the Rendition of Anthony Burns.
III. The Laws of God and the Statutes of Men.
IV. The Dangers which threaten the Rights of Man in America.
V. Some Account of My Ministry.
VI. The Public Function of Woman.
VII. Sermon of Old Age.

SPEECHES, ADDRESSES, AND OCCASIONAL SERMONS.
3 vols. 12mo, cloth. $4.50.

VOL. I.
I. The Relation of Jesus to His Age and the Ages.
II. The True Idea of a Christian Church.
III. A Sermon of War.
IV. A Speech delivered at the Anti-War Meeting in Faneuil Hall.
V. A Sermon of the Mexican War.
VI. A Sermon of the Perishing Classes in Boston.
VII. A Sermon of Merchants.
VIII. A Sermon of the Dangerous Classes in Society.

VOL. II.
I. A Sermon of the Spiritual Condition of Boston.
II. Some Thoughts on the Most Christian Use of Sunday.
III. A Sermon of Immortal Life.
IV. The Public Education of the People.
V. The Political Destination of America, and the Signs of the Times.
VI. A Discourse occasioned by the Death of John Quincy Adams.
VII. A Speech at a Meeting of the American Anti-Slavery Society to celebrate the Abolition of Slavery by the French Republic.
VIII. A Speech at Faneuil Hall before the New-England Anti-Slavery Convention.
IX. Some Thoughts on the Free-Soil Party and the Election of Gen. Taylor.

VOL. III.
I. A **Speech at a** Meeting of the Citizens of Boston in Faneuil Hall, March 25, 1850, to consider the Speech of Mr. Webster.
II. A Speech at the New-England Anti-Slavery Convention in Boston, May 29, 1850.
III. A Discourse occasioned by the Death of the late President Taylor.
IV. The Function and Place of Conscience in Relation to the Laws of Men: a Sermon for the Times.
V. The State of the Nation, considered in a Sermon for Thanksgiving Day.
VI. The Chief Sins of the People.
VII. The Three Chief Safeguards of Society, considered in a Sermon at the Melodeon.
VIII. The Position and Duties of the American Scholar.

CRITICAL AND MISCELLANEOUS WRITINGS. 1 vol. 12mo, cloth. $1.50.

I. A Lesson for the Day.
II. German Literature.
III. The Life of St. Bernard of **Clairvaux.**
IV. Truth against the World.
V. Thoughts on Labor
VI. The Transient and Permanent in **Christianity.**
VII. The Pharisees.
VIII. Education of the Laboring Classes.
IX. How to move the World.
X. Primitive Christianity.
XI. Strauss's Life of Jesus.
XII. Thoughts on Theology.

HISTORIC AMERICANS, — Franklin, Washington, Adams, and Jefferson. With an Introduction by Rev. O. B. Frothingham. $1.50.

These volumes, ten in number, bound in uniform style, are put up in a neat box: price for the set, $15.00.

THE TRIAL OF THEODORE PARKER for the Misdemeanor of a Speech in Faneuil Hall against Kidnapping; with the Defence. 1 vol. 8vo, cloth. $1.50.

THE TWO CHRISTMAS CELEBRATIONS, — A. D. I. and MDCCCLV. A Christmas Story. Square 16mo, cloth. 60 cts.

A SERMON OF IMMORTAL LIFE. Pamphlet, 15 cts.

Sold by Booksellers, or mailed postpaid, on receipt of price, by

HORACE B. FULLER, Publisher,
14 Bromfield Street, Boston.

www.ingramcontent.com/pod-product-compliance
Lightning Source LLC
Chambersburg PA
CBHW020225240426
43672CB00006B/420